you & your **wedding**

The
GROOM'S
Guide

Maia Andrews

foulsham

LONDON • NEW YORK • TORONTO • SYDNEY

foulsham

The Publishing House, Bennetts Close, Cippenham,
Slough, Berkshire, SL1 5AP, England

For Jamie

Foulsham books can be found in all good bookshops and direct from
www.foulsham.com

ISBN-13: 978-0-572-03265-4
ISBN-10: 0-572-03265-X

Printed in China through Colorcraft Ltd, Hong Kong

Cover credit: Daniel Parker 0161 959 0075

Contents

Introduction

Congratulations! The fact that you have picked up
this book probably means you are about to be – or are presently –
caught up in the heady whirlwind of planning a modern
marriage and, more importantly, about to
tie the knot with the girl of your dreams.

It's an encouraging start that you have opened this book and actually taken the brave step of reading the first few lines. Whether you actively purchased it yourself or your bride-to-be thrust it at you with the express instruction to read it from cover to cover before the football starts is neither here nor there; hopefully you'll finish it with a clearer view of your own role in the whole marriage process and a slightly less panicked expression on your face.

The average groom

Having spent a number of years as Grooms Editor of *You & Your Wedding*, the UK's most widely read wedding magazine, I know that, while there are some grooms out there who are taking an active interest in the colour of the flower girl's shoes and can think of nothing better than co-ordinating their tie with their future mother-in-law's handbag, the average groom can feel a wee bit daunted by the whole wedding idea. I'm not talking about doubting your feelings for your fiancée and your intention to marry her – hopefully you gave that your full consideration well before picking up this book. It's more the prospect of dressing up to the nines, spending half the gross national product of a small country, inviting distant relatives to a day-long party where you supply them with booze until your elderly Aunt Aggie falls off her chair, and dealing with the love of your life as she turns from the girl you fell in love with into a stressed-out Bridezilla with a sugared almond habit.

No matter how queasy the prospect of arranging all this makes you feel, the days when all of the wedding planning fell totally to the bride and her family are long gone. In a bygone era a groom could get away with golfing with his mates or hiding away in the pub each weekend chatting about 'manly' topics and current affairs while his wife-to-be ran around frantically organising absolutely everything from the cake to the groom's outfit and getting Daddy dearest to cough up the cash, all while cleaning the house, polishing the silverware and making sure she always had a bow in her hair and a smile on her face at all times – apparently.

Times have moved on though and not every bride has dreamed of her big day from the moment she was born or is happy to shoulder all the responsibility on her own. These days most couples pay some or all of the costs of their own wedding, which means that grooms are much more likely to be involved in the whole process, even if it's just signing some of the cheques. Also, the stereotype of the groom who just wants to sit back, let the bride and her family do all the work and simply turn up on the actual day is just that – a stereotype. There are an equal number of grooms out there who want to have a say in their own wedding day – how it looks, what they wear and who is invited. With this in mind, you can decide what kind of groom you are and exactly what you want from this book. If you simply need bits of information here and there on the specific jobs that are your responsibility, just turn to the appropriate chapters: if you want to have a good idea of everything that is expected from a modern wedding and where you fit into it, start from here and keep going.

Hopefully, with my help and a few essential survival tips, you can begin to allay any fears you have, find out exactly what you need to do and when you need to do it, actively get involved in the parts of the day that you might actually enjoy and ensure that, whatever happens and however stressed your bride-to-be gets, you are there to help her and remind her why she agreed to marry you in the first place. In essence, you will become The Perfect Groom – and have a great time into the bargain. Not bad for less than a tenner.

Now you've already admitted you need a bit of help (it's the first step on the route to a great wedding and nothing to be ashamed of) and you've made it through the introduction, grab yourself a cup of tea – or a beer to make up for missing the football – relax, turn to the first chapter and start to enjoy planning what should be a great day for both you and your bride.

What Style of Wedding?

The first important thing to do after the question has been popped, the engagement champagne has been drunk and both your mothers have cried at the news is to consider the style of your wedding.

Before anything can be booked, you and the missus-to-be have to sit down and imagine your perfect wedding day. Do you want a simple beach ceremony with just the two of you standing next to the lapping surf, or a huge stately home wedding with 250 guests? Will the atmosphere be formal, with waiters, canapé trays and a string quartet, or a casual church hall, no top table and a relaxed dress code?

Religious differences

Different religious beliefs can be a sticking point. If neither of you is particularly religious, then a civil ceremony in a register office or a building, such as a hotel or a stately home, with a room licensed for wedding ceremonies seems to be an obvious choice. If, on the other hand, one of you is religious while the other emphatically is not, or you belong to different religions, you will have to come to some agreement. It is certainly acceptable to have a number of different ceremonies so everyone is happy. For example, if one of you is Church of England and the other Hindu, you could have a quiet civil ceremony to ensure you are legally married, then perhaps a church blessing followed by a Hindu ceremony. Some religions forbid marriages to members of other religions and it is important to check this at an early stage by consulting the respective authorities. If both refuse, a civil ceremony may be necessary for you to be legally married. If you feel this is too restrictive, a civil ceremony can be preceded or followed by a non-religious celebration, which could take place almost anywhere and accommodate almost any wishes you may both have. (See page 136 for contact details of all the religious and civil ceremony organisations.)

Formal or informal?

You'll probably both be comfortable in similar kinds of situations so you may already know the answer to this one. If you enjoy the finer things in life, own your own tuxedo – and wear it regularly – and enjoy being fussed over in posh restaurants, the formal route may be the one for you. Perhaps a castle, stately home or smart London hotel would be the perfect setting. Alternatively, if your style

is a bit more casual, you prefer a good plate of bangers and mash to haute cuisine and plan to let your hair down to some cheesy pop classics before the night is over, a converted barn, local hall, or casual country hotel or restaurant might be a better choice. Whichever you plump for, ensure that your vision of the day and your bride's match up. If not, some kind of compromise will have to be reached.

Feeding the forty thousand or the forty?

You don't need to have a precise guest list at this point but some idea of general numbers will come in very handy. Do you both have a huge extended family, a vast network of friends and numerous work colleagues that you just can't get married without? Or does the thought of standing up in front of hundreds of people fill you with horror and you would both rather keep it small and intimate with just close friends and family – or perhaps even just the two of you? As ever, discussion is the key because you will need to come to a decision about this together.

Budget will also play a major part in this decision as nothing can really be decided until you know how much cash you have to play with. You may want to entertain everyone you've ever met in sumptuous style but if your budget will only stretch to a finger buffet for twenty people you will have to do some serious compromising. Turn to Chapter 2 for the best way to work out what you can afford and how to stick to it.

Setting a date

Do you have a specific date that means a lot to you both or are you prepared to be flexible about the time of year if it means you can have the venue you want? The most popular time of year for weddings is between late spring and early autumn but marrying outside of this time could save you money. It's also worth considering giving yourselves enough time to save up for the wedding if you need to although, however long you have, the wedding planning will expand to take up all the available time – whether it's months, years or decades.

- Spring: you are taking a bit of a chance with the weather but you could be lucky and prices won't be at their highest.

SURVIVAL TIP 1

If discussions are getting heated at this point, take your bride out somewhere under the condition that the wedding is a no-go subject. It should remind you why you popped the question and remind her why she said 'Yes' in the first place. Resume discussions at a later date.

- Summer: high season for weddings because you are more likely to have some sunshine and you can choose warm weather reception options such as marquees and garden parties.
- Autumn: the end of the wedding season when it's easier to book suppliers and venues, although September is still a very popular month.
- Winter: a romantic season to marry, with the early evenings and possibilities for candles and so on. Generally it's also a bit cheaper and since you shouldn't have any expectations about the weather it can't let you down.

Also think about what day of the week you would like your wedding to be on. The current trend is for weekday weddings as they can work out much cheaper than the traditional Saturday wedding, which your venue and a large number of your suppliers will charge a premium for.

What kind of groom are you?

Obviously not all grooms are the same and it's important to establish which category you fall into regarding your impending nuptials and what kind of role you want to play in the whole proceedings. It's also important to determine whether the love of your life is happy with the category you fall into as well – your happiness, not to mention physical wellbeing, may depend on it.

Groom A

You are as laid back as they come and you feel this truly is the bride's day. You are happy to let her plan all the arrangements from the colour theme to the menu and as long as she's happy you are too. If she asks you to do specific things then you are more than willing to help out, but everyone knows that organising is not your strong point, let alone choosing flowers and cake decorations. It's generally assumed that your main job is to turn up at the right time on the right day in the right outfit.

SURVIVAL TIP 2

Sporting fixtures – check these now before committing to a date. You'll have only yourself to blame if six months on you realise that the best day of your life is also the happiest day in your favourite team's career because they're playing in the FA Cup Final, the Rugby World Cup or the last leg of the Extreme Ironing Championships.

Groom B

You are happy to get stuck into the time-honoured male roles of booking the transport and sorting out the honeymoon and you like the sound of finding the band – but table centrepieces and bridesmaids' accessories leave you cold. As far as you are concerned, there is no improving on the traditional allocation of the bride's and groom's roles and she can get on with hers while you happily search the internet for that cool sports car you want to turn up in.

Groom C

You are keen to get involved, as to your mind it's just as much your day as it is the bride's and you want to have a joint say in how your own wedding pans out. You know what you like and actually enjoy discussions about how the tables will look and who gets to sit where as you don't want to turn up on the day not knowing what to expect. You want everything from the flowers to the music to be to your taste as well as your fiancée's and will certainly tell her if you disagree with her ideas. You want the wedding day you end up with to be a combination of both your personal styles.

Support your bride

Whether you are an A, B or C, one of the most important things is to find out how much your bride needs or expects you to be involved.

If you are an A she may love the fact that she gets to make all the important design choices herself and is perfectly capable of dealing with everything. Alternatively, she might require a bit more input from you than 'I don't mind, dear, whatever you think' and start to get stressed out that she's shouldering all the responsibility. If that's the case, try to find a few jobs that appeal to your strengths and interests and which will save her time and effort.

For example, a technically gifted groom could set up an 'Our Wedding' computer file, with all the details of your wedding (timetable of the day, the accommodation, maps, the honeymoon and so on) and a gift list website for your guests to access. If you are good at finances, set up a wedding spreadsheet to keep track of your expenditure and fill it in regularly. Log on to www.youandyourwedding.co.uk and put your details into the budgeter. There's also a seating planner to help sort out your reception tables. Some planning tools will even let you input which guests must not be put near each other! You can then spend many happy hours watching the warning signs flash up when you put Uncle Harry and his ex-wife within two metres of each other.

If you are more of a B then just make sure you and everyone else knows exactly which roles and responsibilities are yours. As long they get done then – hopefully – you can't get yourself into trouble. Keep a check with your bride that she's coping with her responsibilities; the traditional division of wedding tasks favours the guy, so even the most capable fiancée might welcome a helping hand with a few things. But first make sure you've taken complete charge of all your own responsibilities, such as the honeymoon, menswear and transport, then offer help, perhaps by sorting out the photographer or checking that all the legal side of the ceremony has been covered. Maybe set up a spreadsheet to keep track of guests' replies and final guest numbers, or create a good filing system for all the quotes and leaflets you will have gathered and chase suppliers who haven't given you written confirmation – there are plenty of jobs that you can turn your hand to that don't involve ribbons or flowers.

Those of you in the C category will probably spend a fair amount of time explaining to people that you do actually want to help choose the stationery, but don't be deterred; it is your day as much as your bride's and you should be as involved as you want to be. There may be some things that you feel more strongly about than others. For example, if you love your food, then make sure you are involved in choosing the menu; if you are particularly arty or have a good eye for design then there's absolutely no reason why the bride should have all the say in the colour scheme. Grooms are starting to cotton on to the fact that their own wedding day can contain as much fun and excitement for them as it does for the bride and that if there's something they've always wanted to try – within reason – this is the day it will be okayed by the other half. Make sure you take full advantage of this once-in-a-lifetime opportunity and add a few personal touches of your own. It may not be the outfit that gets you excited but if you've always wanted to drive a vintage sports car now is the time to hire one or if you've got a sweet tooth get a chocolate fountain for the reception and spend a happy half an hour dipping away. Make your voice heard and I'm sure your bride will love you for it (as long as you don't veto those cute little heart-shaped placecards she's had her eye on for ages).

Once you've discussed all these important issues – and assuming that the marriage is still on – you should both have a basic idea of how you see your wedding coming together and the style of the big day. You may both have had to compromise in some areas and you may still have to change a few things once the twin influences of both sets of parents are added into the mix but you at least have something to start working with. You can now start thinking about putting together some concrete decisions and even making some firm bookings.

2

The Budget

Whatever your financial situation, discussing
and settling on your wedding budget is fraught with perils
for the unprepared groom.

Traditionally the groom and his family were responsible for paying for the following:

- the bride's engagement and wedding rings
- church fees
- the marriage licence
- the outfits of the male members of the wedding party, including the groom's
- the bride's bouquet and the bridal party's buttonholes and corsages
- gifts for the best man and ushers
- the honeymoon.

This left the poor bride and her family to pick up the tab for everything else, which may not seem like a problem from where you are standing but if you suddenly become a stickler for tradition at this point you won't be fooling anyone.

Nowadays…

… it's more common for couples to be slightly older when they marry. Many have already lived together and also earn enough money to pay for their own wedding. The added bonus of paying for the bulk of it yourselves is that no one can dictate to you what kind of wedding you should have.

You may find that one or both sets of parents are happy to contribute, but this does entitle them to some say in proceedings and they may want to know what their money is being spent on. Alternatively, as much as they may want to, some parents just won't be in a position to contribute much, if anything. Whatever the case, use your common sense when finalising the budget. Don't allocate all your worldly savings so that you have a lavish wedding day but can't afford to eat when you get back from the honeymoon, and be realistic about what family members can afford to contribute.

The price of love

The cost of the average wedding can be astronomical. The latest survey by *You & Your Wedding* magazine put the average cost at nearly £20,000. But before you cancel the wedding and start working out how much sports car you can get with that, don't panic. This is the average and, while many couples spend much more than that, lots of couples have a fabulous day on half that amount or less. Expensive does not necessarily mean good or tasteful, and with a bit of careful budgeting most couples can get the wedding they want for the money available.

Start by working out between you exactly what you can afford to spend. If you are planning to save up for your own wedding, start saving early. Even if you put aside at least £800 per month, to save up that 'average wedding' cost of £20,000 will still take longer than two years. If your budget is less than £2,000, a credit card with a good introductory offer is a sensible choice. For a larger amount, a fixed-interest bank loan may be more cost-effective than your existing credit cards. Then open a specific wedding bank account so you can keep track of your spending and avoid the hassle and possible arguments of working out who has paid for what.

Once you have your total budget, including contributions from family etc., you can start allocating it to different parts of the wedding day and split it into workable sections. The following percentages are intended to give you a rough idea of how much you can expect to spend in each area:

- **Reception: 50%**

  Includes: venue hire, catering, bar bills and beverages, wedding cake and favours

- **Wedding outfits: 10%**

  Includes: bride's dress, accessories, hair and make-up, groom's outfit and attendants' outfits

- **Honeymoon: 15%**

  Includes: honeymoon and first night hotel

- **Music and entertainment: 5%**

  Includes: ceremony musicians, reception musicians and entertainment

- **Flowers: 5%**

  Includes: ceremony flowers, venue flowers, bride's bouquet, bridesmaids' flowers, buttonholes and corsages

- **Photographs and video: 5%**

  Includes: photography, wedding album/prints, video

- **Extras**: 5%

  Includes: wedding rings, registrar or church fees, transport, stationery and gifts

- **Contingency: 5%**

  To cover any unforeseen expenses or anything that goes over budget.

It is unlikely that your wedding budget will cover every single thing you both want so you will probably have to compromise. Start by deciding which areas are most important to you both. If neither of you likes fruit cake but both love live music, ask a

friend or relative to make a simple cake or do away with the cake altogether and spend the money you've saved on a great band. If you'd like to give your guests a free bar but it's too much of a stretch, consider not having favours and put the money you've saved behind the bar instead where it should last for a while.

Ultimately the size of your wedding will determine how big a budget you will need and the easiest way to cut costs is to cut guest numbers. If you're set on a lavish wedding, restrict your numbers to only 50 guests but treat them to a banquet: if it's more important to you both to invite 150 of your friends and family and have a big party, cut costs by serving them a finger buffet rather than a sit-down meal.

Super savers

Other ways to cut costs include:

- Holding a late afternoon ceremony. Not only does this give you both plenty of time to get ready, it also means you save money by only having to feed your guests once during the day.
- Persuading a friend or relative with a nice car to let you use it as the wedding transport.
- Hiring rather than buying outfits for the males in the wedding party. There are some good menswear designers who offer wedding hire so you might want to consider hiring your own outfit as well.
- Choosing flowers that are in season and using plenty of foliage to fill them out. Also, don't leave your ceremony flowers for only the vicar to enjoy; transporting the flowers from your ceremony to your reception venue would save lots of money.
- Having a weekday wedding, which can be a lot cheaper than a Saturday wedding. Also consider getting married outside of the peak May to September period.

- Not inviting children to the reception – but only if that won't cause family ructions.

- Making your own invitations (don't even think of using email for your invitations), or asking a friend with good handwriting to write the menus and placecards.

- Making a CD of your favourite songs to play during the meal; live music is great but not essential and your own compilation can be a nice personal touch.

- Serving your wedding cake instead of a separate dessert.

- Serving bucks fizz to make your champagne go further, or in winter mulled wine is a cheaper drinks option.

- Inviting only close friends and family to the ceremony and wedding breakfast but having a larger party in the evening, which the majority of guests are invited to.

Sticking to your budget

Once your budget has been decided, keep a proper note of what's been spent and if, for example, the dress ends up costing more than predicted you'll have to cut back on what you spend on, say, the flowers. Any number of people from your parents to your florist will try to persuade you to spend more: your aunty may tell you that having no cake is just not the done thing; the caterers may try to insist that the medium-priced menu option is far superior to the basic and you'd be letting everyone down if you didn't go for it.

Ignore them. You know what your budget is and you know what you want, so don't let yourself be bullied into anything else. Better still, avoid any suppliers who try to force you to spend more than you want to; they're meant to be working for you – remember?

You are bound to overspend in some areas but try to keep a tight rein on it, even if you have allowed a small contingency fund. And if you suddenly find yourself or the wife-to-be planning to order an extra-large chocolate fountain, ask yourself if you really need it. Just close your eyes and picture yourselves on a tropical beach on your honeymoon being able to afford that extra glass of rum punch. It will remind you that the money might be better spent elsewhere.

Money matters

The financial side of weddings is possibly the most uninteresting and yet stressful part of planning a wedding and setting up home together, and can be a huge source of conflict. No one really wants to spend hours working out figures but asking a few simple questions may ensure that your married life doesn't begin overshadowed by huge debt and totally differing attitudes to money:

- Are you spenders or savers? And do you both have the same attitudes to money?
- How do you plan to manage your finances once you are married? Do you want to put everything solely in a joint account, or both keep personal accounts too?
- Does one of you plan to retire early while the other wants to go on holiday in style three times a year? It's important to decide whether spending money now or saving for later is the plan.
- How many children do you want? Little bundles of joy can be super expensive, so it's worth planning exactly how much you'll need to save and whether one of you will give up work to look after them.

It might be a difficult thing to have to think about right now, but do remember that if either of you has made a will, the document will be revoked by your marriage. You should make sure you draw up a new one.

Now you've discussed these points and done anything necessary, you can get back to the happy task of planning the wedding – and the rest of your lives – together. And remember: however great the temptation, resist the urge to question whether that isn't an awful lot of money to spend on a dress she will wear only once. It may be true – but she won't want to hear it.

3

The Legal Stuff

Whatever elaborate plans you have for the rest of your day, the ceremony is the part that matters most and is essentially what the whole day is about. Both you and your guests may be looking forward to a slap-up feast, drinking enough booze to sink the Titanic all over again and a performance from the local unicycle club, but before that you will both make some important promises that should last you a lifetime.

The basics

To be legally married in the UK:

- You and your fiancée must be at least 16 years old (in England and Wales, if either of you is under 18, your parents or guardians must give their consent).
- You must not be closely related.
- The marriage must take place in premises where the ceremony can be legally solemnised (register offices, premises licensed for marriages, parish churches and other places of worship registered for marriage).
- The ceremony must take place in the presence of a registrar or authorised person.
- The ceremony must take place between 8 am and 6 pm.
- Two witnesses must be present.
- You must both be free and eligible to marry.

Once you've ticked all those boxes, the next big decision is what type of ceremony you want. If you live in England or Wales, currently you have two main choices:

- A religious ceremony in a church, synagogue or chapel.
- A civil wedding in a licensed building or register office.

In the UK it is not legal to get married in transit, for example on a moving plane, or in places such as a forest or a meadow where no specific address can be given. In Scotland you can hold a civil or religious ceremony anywhere the registrar deems appropriate as it is the registrar him- or herself (rather than the room) who holds the licence. At present there are plans to adopt these rules in England and Wales and a White Paper has been drawn up but it may still be some time before it becomes law. You may have seen pictures of out-of-the-ordinary weddings involving hot air balloons, sky diving and underwater ceremonies, but you need to forget about them if you are marrying in the UK – frankly it's just not British. (See also the information on registrar's general licences on page 29.)

Religious ceremonies

A Church of England wedding

As long as one of you lives in the parish and is on the electoral roll, you should be able to marry in your local church. You don't have to attend church regularly but some ministers may insist on it so check first. The banns – the public announcement of your intention to marry – will be read out in church on three consecutive Sundays, following which the marriage must take place within three months. It is usual for couples to come to church at least once to hear their banns being read. If one party lives in a different parish the banns must be read there too, although not necessarily on the same Sundays.

If the church you want to marry in is outside the parish in which you live and you are not on the electoral roll, you must apply to the Archbishop of Canterbury for a special licence, and you will need to show a long-standing connection with the church and have a good reason to support your application. Just because it's really near your reception venue or it will look good in the photographs is not good enough.

If you are divorced and your former wife is still alive you may find it difficult to have a full marriage service in a Church of England church. Some ministers may make exceptions but it will be judged on a case-by-case basis.

At the time of going to press, current costs for a Church of England wedding are £18 for the publication of your banns and a further £12 for a certificate of banns. The marriage service costs £218 and the marriage certificate £7. If you choose to have bell ringers, charges will vary from church to church, but you can expect to pay an average of about £100. Depending on numbers, a choir can cost anything from £50 to £150 and if you have a soloist then charges will be significantly higher, especially if you want to video their performance. You may also incur costs for church music such as the organist, and possibly a small hire cost; winter weddings may also incur heating costs.

A Roman Catholic wedding

The requirements for a Roman Catholic wedding are much the same as those for a Church of England wedding. Arrange a meeting with your priest as soon as possible and take with you both your baptism and confirmation certificates. Most priests are empowered to act as registrars so the civil aspect of the wedding is also covered.

If you are both Roman Catholic the ceremony is usually part of a Nuptial Mass where you both receive communion, although you may be married with or without a Mass (the full Catholic service). If one of you is not Catholic you will need to obtain a dispensation for a 'mixed marriage', which can usually be granted by your parish priest, and mixed marriages are usually performed outside of the Mass in a ceremony that involves no communion.

The Roman Catholic Church still has strict rules about divorce and does not allow the remarriage of divorcees. Exceptions are made only if your first marriage was not recognised by the Church – but you should consult your priest for advice.

Other religions

For all religious weddings other than Church of England or Roman Catholic, the legal requirements are the same as for civil ceremonies and you will need to apply to the minister or religious authority for your own place of worship as well as the local superintendent registrar. If you want to be married in another area, you will often need to prove you worship regularly or give notice in that area. If you and your fiancée are from different faiths, organising your ceremony might prove a little trickier. Some combination of different ceremonies/blessings may be in order but you need to raise the subject with the ministers involved. See the Useful Contacts list on page 136 for details of different religious organisations.

A blessing

If you have strong religious convictions but can't be married in a church, a blessing, involving the confirmation of your vows, is a good alternative. This can be held after you've had a civil ceremony.

Civil ceremonies

A civil ceremony is conducted by the local registrar, who travels to your chosen venue. The ceremony can have no religious connotations in either the words or music but you can choose to add your own readings, provided they are approved by the registrar. Alternatively, your civil wedding can be held at the local register office.

The first step is for each of you to contact the superintendent registrar for your own district, which you must have lived in for a minimum of seven days. Even if both partners live in the same district, each needs their own superintendent registrar's certificate, so both bride and groom must apply in person to the local office and each is liable for a separate fee. Couples then wait 15 days before the certificates are issued.

At the appointment you will be asked when and where you plan to marry and couples usually book the ceremony at this meeting too, unless they are marrying in a different area, in which case you will probably already have spoken to the superintendent registrar in the district in which you are holding your ceremony.

Civil ceremonies can be held in a register office or any building with a wedding licence, of which there are more than 3,000 at present in England and Wales. Contact your local authority for a list of those in your area or visit www.gro.gov.uk/gro/content/marriages to buy a full list.

It currently costs £30 per person to give notice of your marriage, and fees for a register office wedding can range anywhere between about £150 on weekdays to £430 at weekends. Civil ceremonies at a licensed venue can cost from about £330 during the week to £430 at weekends, although prices vary nationwide. There's also the £7 charge for the marriage certificate.

A registrar's general licence

In special circumstances such as serious illness you can apply for a registrar's general licence, which allows a marriage to take place anywhere at any time and is usually valid for twelve months.

Let's get away from it all

If this already seems far too complicated, another option is to marry abroad. As many as 40,000 UK couples every year now marry overseas and the numbers are steadily rising. There are various worldwide destinations where it is very easy to marry and more and more couples these days can see the attraction of a beach wedding in an idyllic location combined with a smaller number of guests and generally fewer costs. In most of the main destinations for a wedding abroad it is possible to hold a civil or religious ceremony and it can all be arranged by an experienced tour operator. As long as your marriage is legally recognised in the country in which it takes place it is deemed to be valid in the UK, but make sure you do your homework and check with your travel agent. If you are not completely satisfied that your marriage will be legal, pay a visit to your local register office in Britain and they should be able to confirm it for you. Popular places to marry abroad include:

- The Caribbean
- Cyprus
- Greece
- Italy
- Mauritius
- Sri Lanka
- Thailand
- USA.

SURVIVAL TIP 4

If you have loads of relatives who love a free party but hardly know you from Adam, head abroad for your nuptials. You'll find all but your nearest and dearest will be busy that weekend – perfect. Just make it clear who is paying for what, for example, air fares.

However, it is relatively difficult to arrange a wedding in Belgium, Denmark, France, The Netherlands, Norway, Portugal, Russia, Spain or Switzerland.

If you do choose to marry abroad there are a huge number of resorts around the world offering wedding packages for a good price or even included free as part of your stay. Make sure you find out exactly what is included in the price though as extras can often be very expensive. It's also worth finding out how many ceremonies your venue allows in a day as you don't want to feel like you're being hurried through your ceremony to make way for another wedding. Most resorts offer civil ceremonies but many are still able to arrange a religious ceremony. If that's not possible but you have your heart set on a certain place you might want to think about having a religious ceremony at home and then a blessing overseas. Finally, impress your bride by telling her that some airlines will let her hang her dress in the cabin to save it being crushed in the hold. If you're lucky you might be able to get your suit in on the action too. Ask when you book.

The ceremony

Once you are sure all the legalities are covered you can add personal touches, with both words and music, to a religious or civil ceremony to make it your own. Your choices should reflect your personalities as well as your style and your relationship. If you have a song that reminds you of when you first met or a special moment in your lives together then consider including it, along with a meaningful poem or reading. You should perhaps reconsider, though, if you find yourself composing a 24-verse epic with a blow-by-blow account of your love and adoration for each other; it's a fine line between sentimental and slushy. Equally, if you are more the stiff-upper-lip specimen of British manhood, there are a great number of readings that are sweet and appropriate but won't require your guests to bring extra tissues. You have to work within the guidelines laid down by law, so make sure you check every step of the way with your minister or registrar, who will have the final say over everything you want to include.

I vow to thee

There is also scope to change your marriage vows, should you want to. There is less flexibility with a religious ceremony but you may be allowed to add something extra; and, if either of you are uncomfortable with a particular phrase, speak to your minister about a possible

SURVIVAL TIP 5

She won't promise to obey you. Don't be tempted to ask.

change. Many modern brides prefer to say 'love, honour and cherish' rather than promising to 'obey' while, luckily for you, instead of only the husband promising to bestow all his worldly goods on his new spouse, it is more usual for you both to promise it.

The music for a church wedding is traditionally provided by the organist and you should ask to hear him or her play before you book their services. Also, don't feel you have to have traditional tunes just because it's a traditional church wedding; you may want to have some contemporary music for the bride's arrival, the signing of the register and/or the recessional.

Let's be civil

Legally, a civil wedding can't have vows, songs, poems or readings with religious references. The exact content is at the registrar's discretion but can even exclude songs or readings that mention the word 'soul', for example, although some registrars may allow it providing the context is not explicitly religious. You generally won't be allowed to include anything that extends the ceremony beyond a total of 15 to 20 minutes. If you need help finding appropriate readings, head to your local bookshop to find books packed with vows and readings suitable for weddings. You can also take inspiration from your favourite films, songs and novels, all of which might have something to inspire you.

The right music for your civil ceremony can heighten the drama of the bride's entrance (which may or may not be good for you waiting nervously at the front), provide a nice pause and maintain the mood during the signing of the register. A register office ceremony tends to be shorter and simpler than a church service and there may not be time for any musical accompaniment during the ceremony; some register offices don't even have a CD player so if this is important to you make sure you check it out in advance.

As long as your music has no religious connotations then the world is your oyster, although if your favourite song is Iron Maiden's *Bring Your Daughter to the Slaughter* you may want to picture how your grandmother might react to that as well as the seriousness of the occasion and opt for something slightly more suitable. There'll be plenty of time for all your favourite tunes later on in the day if they're more suited to the dance floor than the ceremony.

Freedom of speech

At the moment the only way to have total freedom of expression is at a Humanist ceremony. This won't be legally recognised so it must be preceded by a civil ceremony. Humanist ceremonies can be held wherever you choose, from your back garden to a beach or hot air balloon. A friend or family member can oversee proceedings or you can hire a celebrant. Contact the British Humanist Association (see page 136) for more advice.

The Wedding Party

It is best not to underestimate the importance of the rest of the wedding party. During the ups and downs of planning your wedding you may come to rely on some of your close friends and family a little more than any of you have been used to – whether for simple things such as ironing your shirt on the morning of the wedding or finding your car keys to getting you off the Edinburgh sleeper after your stag night and pouring you into a cab.

The best man

Choosing the right best man can be a difficult task. The best man has quite a few important responsibilities to deal with before the wedding and on the big day itself and it's not a job to be taken lightly. His main roles are the following:

- organise the stag night
- help you with your responsibilities, such as transport and menswear
- accompany you to the ceremony
- look after the rings on the day
- introduce the speeches at the wedding breakfast if you don't have a toastmaster
- dance with the chief bridesmaid after the first dance
- settle any outstanding bills on the day, such as taxi fares or the band's fee
- return any hired outfits after the wedding
- and last, but certainly not least, give a rip-roaring best man's speech.

On top of all that, he generally has to lend a hand wherever necessary, organise the ushers, look after any problems that may arise, get people together for the photographs at the reception, mingle with guests, dance with any female relatives who look like they're dying for a spin on the dance floor, help tidy up at the end and try not to get too drunk – at least until after his speech.

Above all the best man's job is a supportive one, so don't ask anyone who can be a bit unreliable or disorganised or who is simply very busy. It may be best not to choose someone you know is very shy, as the prospect of giving a speech may mean he gets no sleep for months before the wedding. Also, no matter how close a friend he is now, don't ask anyone who has had a previous relationship with the bride – it might be a bit weird.

If your problem is that you have too many good candidates for the job, why not have two best men? They can organise the stag night together and then divide up the wedding day jobs. They could even give the speech as more of a double act. Alternatively, you may want a sister or a close female friend to be your best 'man'. The tradition of the best man came about in a time when it was considered unseemly to have friends of the opposite sex before marriage: in this day and age it's obviously the norm. But make sure your bride is in agreement before you ask a female friend – she may not be keen on having another woman share the altar on her big day; equally she may be perfectly happy with it and even choose to be supported by a male usher instead of a bridesmaid.

Ushers

If you have other close friends that you would like to involve in the wedding party, they can be given another important role on the day as an usher. The ushers are responsible for showing people to their seats, giving out the orders of service or hymn books, and generally helping out the best man at the reception shepherding guests in the right direction and so on. It's a nice way to include a few more of your friends or relatives in the big day.

The chief bridesmaid

The chief bridesmaid, normally your bride-to-be's closest friend, may be your saving grace on a number of occasions. Officially her role is to support the bride in any way she can, particularly any areas that you are proving deficient in, such as choosing flowers and dresses. Before the wedding she will need to help choose her own outfit and attend any necessary fittings, help the bride with any part of the planning she needs and generally supply a shoulder to cry on and a glass of wine if it all gets too much. Her main responsibility is to organise a hen night to send off your bride in style; this may involve anything from a long weekend in Barcelona to tank driving in Wales or hardcore clubbing in any number of major cities around the UK. It will almost definitely involve comedy outfits, drunken forfeits and a few photographs that you will never see – this is for the best. The less you can be involved in this side of things the better but you may be roped in by the chief bridesmaid at some point to provide childhood photographs, anecdotes or embarrassing underwear for the sole purpose of humiliating the bride. Be certain that your bride will see the funny side before handing over anything intimate or too revealing – remember she hasn't signed the marriage certificate yet.

On the big day the chief bridesmaid will normally help the bride get ready in the morning and take charge of any flower girls or younger bridesmaids who need supervising. During the ceremony she looks after the bride's bouquet and often helps her push her veil back. It is becoming more common for the chief bridesmaid to give a speech at the reception, if the bride would like her to, and she should help the best man mingle with the guests and check that everyone is having a good time. Her final job is to join you and your new wife on the dance floor with the best man after your first dance.

SURVIVAL TIP 6

Stay on good terms with the chief bridesmaid. She may tip you off about things you are supposed to have done but haven't – before the bride finds out and gets really cross about it.

Flower girls/pageboys

Younger attendants – known as flower girls and pageboys – are usually the children of close friends or relatives. Their main job is to look cute and, if at all possible, not to cry or run around during the ceremony. They should be put under the watchful eye of one of the other adult attendants and hopefully not cross your field of vision too often.

Father of the bride

Hopefully you will already have a fairly good relationship with the father of the bride, having asked him for his daughter's hand in marriage. Traditionally during the marriage ceremony his role was to 'give away' his daughter to her new husband. These days most brides prefer to play down the giving away side of things but most still choose to walk down the aisle on his arm. The father of the bride may also be coughing up large

amounts of cash for the day, and the combination of 'losing' a daughter and half his pension fund in one go may make it an emotional day for him.

At the ceremony he speaks first and offers a few words of welcome to the guests before introducing his new son-in-law. Later on, following the first dance, the father of the bride and the groom's mother might take a turn on the dance floor to seal family relationships, along with the groom's father and the bride's mother, but equally the bride might choose to dance the second dance of the night with her father.

Father of the groom

Your father doesn't really have any major responsibilities at the wedding. He sits on the top table and wears the same outfit as the rest of the men in the wedding party. It is not unheard of for him to stand up and say a few words during the speeches if he wants to, to welcome the bride into the family.

Mother of the bride

As much as you may consider the wedding day to be yours and your fiancée's, the mother of the bride may also think of it as partly her day. She may have been looking forward to it almost as much as the bride as it's a chance for her to dress up to the nines and entertain her family and friends. While she has no specific roles as such, it is likely that she will have played a big role in getting the venue ready and she will usually spend the morning with the bride helping her to get ready before travelling to the ceremony with the bridesmaids.

It may well be to your advantage to check throughout the day that your new mother-in-law is having a good time; if she is unhappy you may not know about it at the time – but could spend the rest of your life paying for it.

Mother of the groom

That last piece of advice applies equally to your own mother. Don't let her think that you are paying more attention to the mother of the bride, and woe betide you if you don't get both of them exactly the same-sized thank-you bouquet. Unless you know for certain that they are already discussing between themselves what they will be wearing on the day, it will pay to liaise with both mothers. It may be the last thing on your mind but if they both turn up in the same delicate shade of mauve there'll be hell to pay. Traditionally the mother of the bride has precedence over what colour she chooses.

Witnesses

Legally you need two competent adults to witness your marriage and sign their names in the register, and in the eyes of the law these are the two most important people after the bride and groom. If there is someone you would like to include in your wedding day who doesn't fit into any of the traditional roles, such as a step-parent, grandparent, close friend or uncle, it might be nice to offer them the job. It may be diplomatic to ask someone from each side, such as the two mothers or one of your siblings and one of your bride's.

Tricky family situations

If your or your bride's parents are divorced and you want to include any new partners they have in the planning of the day, perhaps delegate a few important jobs to them. Maybe your stepmother can sort out the flowers and your stepfather look into wedding transport for you? That way everyone feels included. There's also no need to have a top table if family situations will make it a bit complicated or divorced parents just don't get on. The aim is for you two to have a stress-free day, and if that means having just the two of you on a table together then that's the best plan.

Reaping the rewards

There are tons of rewards for being part of the main wedding party. You get to share in one of the most special days of your friends' lives, you get a brand new outfit and you get lots of respect from all the other guests. To top it all off, you are supposed to get a gift too. Traditionally gifts are given to the bridesmaids, the mothers of the bride and the groom, the ushers and best man, and anyone else who's been particularly helpful in organising your day. As the groom you are particularly responsible for choosing gifts for your best man and ushers, though if you are lucky you will get a

helping hand from your bride. A nice bouquet of flowers is normally appropriate for both mothers, and this is given in the spirit of 'thanks for being my mum' rather than for any particular role they have played in organising the day.

You don't have to be particularly lavish with your presents for the ushers and best man, but a pair of cufflinks engraved with a message or the wedding date makes a nice gift. Another traditional choice is an engraved hip flask or even a watch. If those don't really inspire you, some other ideas are:

- a few shares in his favourite football club
- membership of a beer club that will send him a selection of beers every month for a year
- a day out racing
- an MP3 player pre-loaded with a selection of cool tunes
- a bottle of really good wine that he can lay down for while
- Tickets to a football/cricket/rugby match
- any kind of shiny electronic gadget.

There are no rules as to what you should give – simply use your imagination!

A gift for the bride

You may be under the impression that you are already giving quite a lot to the bride, such as her engagement ring, her wedding ring, the remainder of your life… Think again. You are supposed to ensure she receives a gift from you for the morning of the wedding. Make a strong mental note of this as it would be terrible to be getting everything right up until the morning of the big day and for it then to go pear-shaped. As it's deemed unlucky for you both to see each other at this time, ask a member of the wedding party to give the bride your gift.

Traditionally a piece of jewellery always goes down well, and even better than a piece of jewellery is a piece of jewellery with lovely big diamonds on. Don't panic though if this is well out of your, by now, dwindling budget. Your bride has come this far so she will know what you can and can't afford. If diamonds are out of the question, then something that shows a bit of thought and consideration is worth more than any amount of money. A necklace or bracelet engraved with a romantic phrase or the date of the wedding should be equally well received.

Making a Guest List and Finding a Venue

Deciding who should be invited to share your big day, and then finding the right, affordable, venue to put them all in, on the day and at the time you want, are issues fraught with difficulties and possible conflicts. The advantages of a foreign beach wedding, with just two hotel employees as your witnesses, may start to become all too apparent!

The guest list

It's best to start with a list of everyone you would invite if you had millions in the bank and plenty of space to spare. Divide it into three sections:

- must-haves
- would-likes
- possibles.

Both sets of parents may also have a view on who they think should be there. Technically you don't have to invite anyone you don't want to but if both your parents are contributing to the cost of the wedding – especially if they are paying for the majority of it – that should give them some say in the guest list. This is where disagreements might occur, with parents feeling entitled to invite their friends while you want to include all your mates. If space is limited, you will just have to be strict; or, if it comes down to cost, you could perhaps offer to pay an extra contribution yourselves for a few more guests. Tread carefully.

Your budget will play an important part in the size of your guest list. Unless you are the aforementioned millionaire (in which case that's it, job done, just invite the whole list!), your initial list will have to be cut slightly or even considerably. As a very general rule, approximately 80 per cent of the people you invite will attend but don't rely on this and invite more people than you can cater for – they just might all turn up.

Little blighters

An easy way to cut down your guest list is not to invite any children. A lot of couples would prefer not to have children there anyway, but obviously this may make it impossible for some people to attend if they are unable to get babysitters or the wedding is a long way from home. It is generally accepted that if children's names are not on the invitation they are not included, though a personal

phone call to explain might be appropriate. Make sure it's a blanket ban (perhaps even consider having a minimum age), otherwise people will be justifiably upset to see other people's kids chomping their way through the wedding cake when their precious offspring have been left at home. If this is going to be your rule, try not to make exceptions for anyone unless you really have to.

Trimming the numbers

After that it gets a bit trickier to cut numbers. If you really have to make more cutbacks, consider the following:

- any of your friends'/relatives' boyfriends and girlfriends that you've never met
- distant work colleagues
- relatives and cousins you rarely see
- any relatives you feel obliged to invite because you went to their wedding.

Evening all

If you can't bear to be quite that harsh and your list is still far too long, another alternative is to invite only very close friends and family to the ceremony and meal and have a bigger evening party for the rest of the guests.

Choosing a venue: the right place at the right time

Once you've settled on a rough idea of numbers, you've armed yourselves with the two most important bits of information – how much you can afford and how many people you want to spend it on. You may already have a special date in mind and a local church and nearby venue. If not, it may be a case of spending a few too many evenings driving around your local area chatting to wedding co-ordinators at different venues. After the fifth or sixth one

you'll probably be reaching breaking point so try to eliminate unnecessary visits by finding out beforehand:

- whether the venue has a wedding licence, if you are planning a civil ceremony there
- if it can cater for the number of guests you have in mind
- if it is free on the date/dates you are after (popular venues can be booked up to a year in advance)
- a rough idea of costs, such as the venue hire charge, the cost per head for catering and maybe room charges if applicable.

Between you, make a list of all the other things that are important for you in your ideal venue. Should it have room for guests to stay over? Do you want a late licence? Is there a golf course nearby for a quick, calming game before the wedding?

SURVIVAL TIP 7

Even if having a golf course handy comes high on your list of priorities, don't tell the bride. As far as she's concerned, it shouldn't come any higher than at least number 25.

The internet can be an invaluable tool and tell you everything you need to know from the comfort of your own home as most venues these days have comprehensive websites with photographs, price details and contact information. Also, before you commit to a two-hour appointment in the back of beyond, ask for a wedding brochure to be sent. This will normally contain things such as details of the rooms available, sample menus and accommodation packages. One important thing to bear in mind if you are holding your ceremony in a different venue to the reception, is that the two should ideally be no more than 20 minutes' drive apart to save yourselves and your guests too much travelling time.

Recommendations from friends and family are always a good starting point, or think about places that you've been to as a wedding guest. If you want a traditional sit-down wedding breakfast, you need to have a fairly large function room compared to a buffet reception for the same number of guests. For a winter wedding, you may also need another room to hold the drinks reception in. There are plenty of unusual places to hold your reception, from zoos to museums, castles to concert halls and Tower Bridge to the London Eye. Hopefully you won't have to visit all of them before you find the perfect one.

A historic stately home

These can be very lavish but also very expensive, and are normally suited to formal sit-down dinners with large numbers of guests. They tend to be well organised, with on-site co-ordinators who will probably save you tons of time, effort and stress. However, not great if you are planning one hell of a knees-up and you can't trust your best man not to be sick in the fountain.

The local church hall

A church hall reception allows guests to spill straight out of the church and into the reception venue and can be great if you are on a tight budget. Decorations may need a fair amount of work and planning, and be prepared to hire everything you need from tables and chairs to glassware. It's also worth making an effort to dress the hall up, otherwise it may be a bit too reminiscent of the local youth club disco you went to when you were 14.

A restaurant

Lots of restaurants have private rooms available for hire, which can be great for a small wedding. Choose one with the right atmosphere and style and it will be practically ready to go straight away.

A hotel

Hotels are suited to most styles of wedding; simply pick one with the right ambience and look. Hotels that offer wedding receptions will be used to taking charge of the proceedings too and most will offer a wedding package including food and drinks, with a price per head and generally a charge for room hire so it should be clear what the total cost will be. An added bonus is that you can stumble into bed in the hotel after the reception.

A marquee

If you want your wedding to be at home or at a parent's house, a marquee can't be beaten, although they can be an expensive option as you'll need to hire all your cutlery and furniture as well things like heaters and portaloos. On the plus side, it means that you can make all the rules about how long the reception lasts, how loud the music is and so on.

Before booking make sure you ask your venue the following…

- Is there on-site catering? Can we bring our own caterers?
- Do we need to hire tables, chairs, linens or tableware?
- What is the basic cost of hiring the venue? What are the extras?
- How much time is included in the rental period?
- Is everything fully insured?
- Will there be other functions on the same day as ours?
- Can we use the gardens? Is there room for a marquee?
- Is there scope to decorate the reception rooms?
- Is there a bridal suite and can guests stay overnight?
- Are there any restrictions on candles, smoking etc?

Something a bit different

There are plenty of quirkier options, but only you know what the response will be when you suggest marrying at your favourite football team's grounds – so at your own risk be it. Premiership football grounds aside, you can also get married anywhere that holds a licence – from museums and art galleries to moored boats and theme parks. There may be restrictions on things like dancing and candles if you book an art gallery, for example, and you obviously can't hold a wedding for 150 guests in a capsule on the London Eye – but you'll definitely give your guests a wedding to remember.

6

What to Wear

There are endless possibilities these days for the groom
and the other men in the wedding party. Wedding wear no
longer simply means morning dress and actually you probably
have almost as much choice as the bride – after all, most brides
still opt for a dress at the white end of the colour spectrum.
You, on the other hand, can go for practically any colour suit in
a variety of styles and then accessorise with waistcoats, handkerchiefs
or even a top hat and cane should you feel like it.

Morningwear

Morningwear, still the most popular choice for the groom, traditionally consists of grey striped trousers, a black, grey or navy single-breasted tailcoat, wing collar shirt, silk tie or cravat and sometimes a top hat, which is not worn but carried in the left hand. Morningwear can be given a more modern touch by having matching trousers and jacket. It's most appropriate for church weddings and civil weddings in a fairly formal setting and can look very flattering on the majority of figures.

Lounge suit

If you don't fancy the idea of getting trussed up in something unlike anything you normally wear, a lounge suit may be a better option. It's perhaps most suited to contemporary, relaxed civil weddings but there's no reason why a lounge suit can't be appropriate for a religious wedding too. There's also the added bonus that if you decide not to hire it you will be left with a great suit that you can wear time and time again after the big day.

Black tie

Black tie consists of a tuxedo and matching bow tie and is most suited to evening weddings in fairly formal surroundings. Bear in mind that if you are in black tie it's usual for your male guests to wear it too, along with evening dresses for the ladies. You can even go one step further and opt for white tie, if you really fancy a certain kind of James Bond elegance.

Frock coat

Frock coats can be plain, patterned brocade, velvet or silk jackets, which generally reach down to mid-thigh, with standard or Nehru collars – they have a slight Edwardian dandy look about them. They are worn with plain black

trousers and a cravat and are proving a popular choice for today's groom, perhaps because they fall somewhere between the traditional tailcoat and the modern lounge suit in style.

Military uniform

Many grooms who are full-time members of the armed forces choose to wear their regimental uniforms. The traditional uniform for a wedding is the Blues uniform: a blue jacket with a high collar. The jacket is teamed with matching blue trousers with a red stripe down the side, accessorised with white belt and gloves.

Highland dress

Scottish grooms often wear Highland morning or evening dress, including a kilt, Prince Charlie jacket or doublet, a sporran, laced brogues, socks, bow tie and a *sgian dubh* – a small dagger worn in the sock.

Accessories

This may be the first time in your life that you've consciously accessorised something, but it's not as daunting as it sounds. The main options are the following:

Waistcoats

The standard option with waistcoats is to hire them along with the rest of your outfit. There are endless colour options to choose from and normally the groom and his attendants wear matching waistcoats that complement the colour theme of the wedding.

If you want something a bit special, you can buy your own waistcoat or have one hand-made to a pattern and in the fabric of your choice or with your names and wedding date embroidered on it. If you really want to do something romantic that will win her over for ever, have her name or 'Lucky Man' embroidered on the back for all to see when you remove your jacket for the evening. The brownie points gained will be incalculable! Also, remember to leave the bottom button of your waistcoat undone, it's tradition – and one you will appreciate after a three-course meal and a few drinks.

Shoes

Don't pass up this opportunity to kit yourself out with a great pair of smart shoes – if you receive complaints from the bride remind her gently that at least you can wear these again. If you are wearing morning dress it's traditional to wear shiny black leather shoes. If you are wearing a lounge suit you can choose whatever colour is most appropriate – black, brown, blue or even pink. A smart white suit with white leather shoes can look great but avoid anything that looks tacky.

What to Wear

SURVIVAL TIP 8

Clean your shoes before the wedding but, and it's a big but, make sure you get ALL the polish off. Black shoe polish stains across the bottom of your bride's sumptuous silk train will not be appreciated.

Ties

There are a number of different tie options: the standard tie, which can be tied in different ways depending on the size of the knot you want; the cravat, which is normally worn with morningwear; or the bow tie, usually worn at more formal evening weddings. Whichever option you choose, make sure you or someone in the wedding party learns how to tie it properly before the morning of the wedding.

Cufflinks

If being trussed up to the nines is not your normal look, cufflinks are a great way to show a bit of personality and there is no end to the style options. You can use them to pay homage to your favourite team or hobby, or have ones with your wedding date engraved on them or even a pair made featuring a picture of your bride-to-be. They also make great presents for your best man and ushers.

Hats

Top hats are not as popular at modern weddings as they once were but if you want that super-smart look then they can't be beaten – you'll also be able to get that great classic shot of all the men in the wedding party throwing their hats in the air and cheering. They're widely available to hire for all the wedding party or you can blow the budget and treat yourself to your own hat from a specialist hat company – although what you could do with it after the wedding is anybody's guess. Put keepsakes in it?

Hiring your suits

If you are hiring suits for yourself and the wedding party don't leave it too late. The details should be organised at least two months before the date of the wedding, particularly if you are marrying in the peak wedding season (May to September). Most hire companies will have your outfits ready a week to ten days before the wedding so that you can have a final fitting and check you have all the correct sizes. Don't leave this until the day before the wedding, when it will be too late to get replacements. Hired outfits are normally returned the first working day after the wedding and this is generally a job for the best man. Most hire companies offer an accidental damage waiver that it's worth taking up just in case the best man opts for some late night break-dancing in his flash suit. Take extra care if you are hiring top hats though, as they are often not covered by this because so many groomsmen lose them. Turn to page 135 for a list of menswear companies.

Buying your suit

Even if you are buying your suit off-the-peg it's still advisable to start looking well in advance and definitely have something bought at least two months before the wedding. You'll need to know what you are wearing before

you can order the suits for the rest of the male wedding party. A suit that is tailored to fit you can take up to a month to be finished, while a suit that's purpose made just for you can take two months or more.

Sartorial faux pas

There are loads of potential sartorial pitfalls for the ill-prepared groom. Commit the following to memory and you should get though the minefield unscathed:

- Don't wear your Donald Duck socks. This is definitely the day to leave comedy items of clothing at home.
- Make sure you give your new shirt a wash so it doesn't have that straight-from-the-pack look about it.
- Ask your best man to carry a spare pair of plain cufflinks. Someone is bound to turn up without any.
- If you are getting ready at the hotel DO NOT use the hotel's steam iron. If it leaves any rust marks or a crease that's impossible to shift you'll be in trouble.
- Remember to take the price labels off your new shoes and wear them in slightly – you don't want to find you can't make that first dance because of blisters. Score the soles lightly with a knife, or roughen them up with sandpaper, so they have some grip on that polished church floor.
- Remember that men wear their buttonhole on the left lapel, the same side as their handkerchief, while women wear theirs on the right.

Stay on target

If you fancy toning up a bit and doing away with those love handles, at least six months before the wedding is the time to start working on it. Join a gym and get a programme specially tailored for you to target any bits you are not happy with. But remember that she's already agreed to marry you so no drastic changes are required. Also, if you are planning to shed a few pounds, make sure you consider this when ordering your suit.

Your wedding day can prove to be a handy goal if there are a few things you've been meaning to change, such as losing weight, giving up smoking or eating more healthily. Remember not to overdo it and don't try to do all the above at the same time – be realistic about what you can achieve.

Grooming the groom

Step back and take a long hard look at yourself. You can't be doing too badly as you've managed to persuade some lovely lady to marry you, but could you do with a bit of a scrub up for the big day? Does your grooming 'regime', if you can call it that, simply consist of splash of water and a dab of soap?

Moisturise, moisturise, moisturise

Now don't be scared; moisturiser is not a dirty word, and you may find that, rather than ridiculing you and ostracising you from their social circle, a number of your mates use it on the quiet. A little bit of grooming before the big day won't go amiss, but if you're not quite ready to start having facials and waxes simply getting yourself a better brand

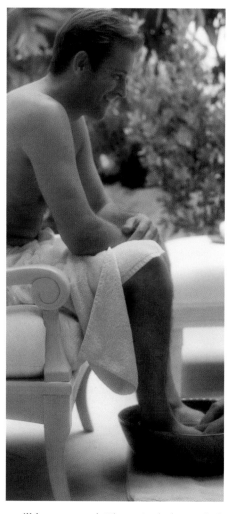

of face soap and a good men's moisturiser may be enough to give your skin that extra something.

If you don't find the idea of a facial totally abhorrent, it may well be worth visiting one of the new men's spas springing up around the country. They're not all pink fluffy gowns and essence of petunia: the new trend is for totally male-friendly places where you can watch sport, get a haircut, have a beer or a good whisky while reading the newspaper and at the same visit some lovely lady who will massage your shoulders and make your skin look like a newborn's. Imagine if they offered that kind of service down your local pub?

And while you are at it, there will never be a better time to try your first proper shave. You could even book one for the morning of the wedding, as once you've tried it

you'll be converted. It's particularly good if you are prone to five o'clock shadow and – more than that – it's a deeply relaxing experience that should help to calm any pre-wedding nerves. One note of caution: if you have particularly sensitive skin, be wary of applying anything new just before the wedding just in case you have a bad reaction to it. Tomato-coloured skin is not a good look this season!

Hit the nails on the head

On your wedding day your hands, and more importantly your fingernails, will be scrutinized more than on any other day in your entire life as everyone tries to get a look at your new wedding ring. A manicure is a really good idea to get them into decent shape but if the idea of this, on top of the moisturiser, is just too much at least make sure they are clean and your nails are trimmed.

Hair today

If you are considering a change of haircut, the week before the wedding is not the time to experiment. See your hairdresser at least three months before to try out a new style – if you are happy with it he or she will be able to do it again nearer the time: if you are not, there's plenty of time for it to grow back again. Don't be tempted to surprise your bride on the big day with a new look; remember, those photographs will be with you FOR EVER.

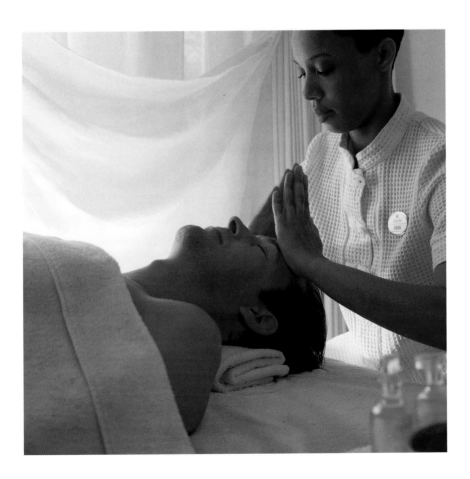

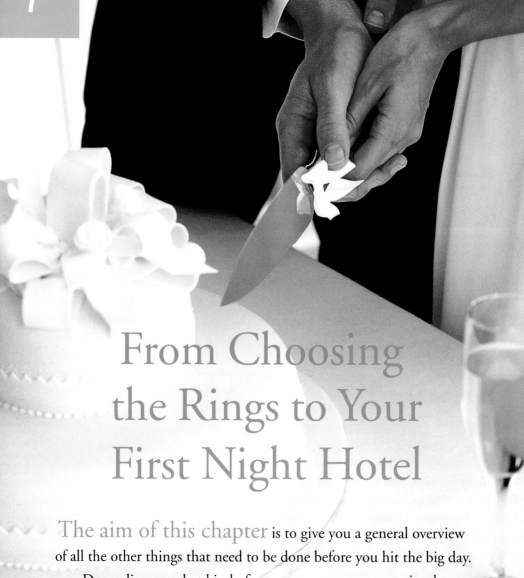

7

From Choosing the Rings to Your First Night Hotel

The aim of this chapter is to give you a general overview
of all the other things that need to be done before you hit the big day.
Depending on what kind of groom you are, you may simply
skim-read the headings, come over a little faint and then decide
to read the paper instead. Or, you may get a little
further and start to delve into a few of the tasks that really interest
you – while pointing out to your fiancée any she needs to do.
Alternatively, you may read this chapter from start to finish,
make notes in the margins and perhaps even create a comprehensive
spreadsheet to fill in as all the jobs progress.

Whichever category you fall into, this chapter includes everything a groom could need to know about a modern wedding – even the very traditionally non-male jobs. You never know, something might catch your eye that you've never taken an interest in before or frankly never had a clue existed. At the very least, when your fiancée asks you will be able to reel off a list of all the jobs as if you've taken a deep interest. She'll be very impressed and start telling her girlfriends that, even though you pretend not to be too bothered with this wedding planning lark, you are actually an old romantic softie at heart. It can't hurt – unless she starts to tell *your* mates about it.

The caterers

This may mean the catering staff at your venue or you may be hiring in outside caterers. The three main wedding options are a drinks and canapés reception, a seated buffet, or a formal sit-down meal. Whichever option you choose, chances are if your venue is doing the catering you will have a set package with a price per head. The catering is likely to be one of your biggest expenses but it should be fairly easy to estimate accurately how much it will set you back. Do make sure you try the food at the venue first so you can make an informed choice about it (and get some free grub into the bargain!).

If your venue isn't doing the catering it may insist you use one of its suppliers but if not, or you are at home or in a marquee, there are tons of great caterers out there that should be able to supply exactly what you want.

Drinks may also be included in your package, but if not you may be able to save money by bringing your own alcohol and paying a corkage fee (for the venue staff to open the bottles). If you decide to do this, it is probably worth making a day trip to France and stocking up because you can make massive savings and, as long as it's for your own consumption and you won't be selling it, there is almost no limit to how much you can bring back. On average, you will need to allow for one to two glasses of sherry, champagne or wine for each guest as an aperitif.

During the meal allocate each guest three to four glasses of wine, and one to two glasses of champagne as well as between half a litre and one litre of soft drinks. You'll probably be able to get 6 to 8 glasses out of each bottle of champagne or wine and 10 to 12 glasses from a bottle of sherry.

The type of food you serve and the number of guests will also influence how much booze you will need, as well as the length of the reception. If your wedding is at noon and the reception goes on until midnight you are going to get through a fair amount unless you have a disproportionate number of teetotallers among your friends and family.

The photographs

After finding your venue, booking your photographer is one of the first things that needs to be done as the best ones are busy months, or even years, in advance. Your venue may be able to recommend some good local photographers, who will have the added advantage of having worked at the venue before and will know the most photogenic spots. Otherwise, wedding magazines such as *You & Your Wedding*, the internet, local newspapers, the Yellow Pages or recommendations from family and friends are good places to start.

Make sure you see a few different photographers' albums and check that you are not looking at single shots from twenty different weddings. Albums like that are easy to compile: the sign of a good photographer is consistently good shots from the same wedding. The other important thing to know about wedding photography is that it can take up a huge amount of your wedding budget – about 5 per cent is a good estimate – and the best wedding photographers can charge thousands. While you don't have to spend that much, don't be tempted to scrimp; the photos are the one thing you are left with after all the cake's been eaten so you'll want something good to remind you of your wedding day.

When comparing prices, ask your photographer for a breakdown of the costs. The price normally depends on three main factors: how long the photographer spends at your wedding; the number of pictures taken; and the type of album. Sometimes paying a little bit extra means you get to keep the proofs of your pictures, which might be worth more in the long run. You may also pay a lower price if you choose not to have pictures taken of the bride getting ready at home or if you agree that the photographer will leave before the reception starts. Decide what's most important to you and what you can live without.

It's a good plan to spend a decent amount on your main

photographer but if there's some money to spare a professional videographer is also a good idea. Everyone's seen friends' cheesy wedding videos, all shot in soft focus and set to the dulcet tones of the chart-topping diva of the day – and thought better of it later. These days there's a wealth of other options. Forget the soft focus and 1980s love songs, quality videographers can make your wedding look like a Hollywood movie. You can even have a spoof documentary made by a professional documentary maker or opt to go back in time and have the whole thing shot on cine film, which has a beautiful kitsch quality to it. Yes, you can always get your mate with a video camera to shoot it instead but the results, while nice to have, will probably not be something you will want to watch very often.

Doing it yourself

Putting a single-use camera on each table at the reception is a great way of making sure you get at least one shot of every single person at the wedding (it is also a good way of making sure that you get over a hundred pictures that are absolutely appalling and perhaps twenty that are real gems). Hopefully it will be worth it for the few good ones and they are a great way for your guests to break the ice. Most disposable camera wedding sets come with developing already included, so they are fairly simple to get developed and won't land you with a huge bill after the wedding.

Wedding stationery

This encompasses a whole heap of things and not just the invites. It includes:

- invitations, plus everything associated with them such as reply cards and maps
- orders of service
- menus
- placecards
- a tableplan
- thank-you cards.

It is generally accepted that the style of your invitations sets the tone for your day, giving people a clue as to how formal or informal it's going to be. For example:

- stiff cards with elegant formal lettering embossed in gold = formal
- comedy caricatures of the pair of you standing on the beach where you got engaged = informal.

There are countless stationery companies out there vying for your business with an endless range of designs, so it shouldn't be a problem finding something you like. Alternatively, you may decide to make your own. This is a perfectly good option if you have plenty of time, a decent amount of artistic skill between you and lots of helpful mates who will lend a hand, and it will most certainly save you money. On the other hand, if you know you are both a little disorganised, you have less than six months to go and most of your friends have suddenly developed a curious allergy to Pritt Stick, it's probably best to leave it to the professionals.

The only other thing that can be a bit tricky with your invitations is the wording. Traditionally, and if they are paying for the bulk of the wedding, the invites are sent from the bride's parents. If you are paying for most of the wedding yourselves the invites are from the two of you. If the hosting parents are divorced or remarried or you have a widowed parent as host this should be reflected in the invitation wording. Your stationer should be able to advise you on the correct format to use.

Also included with the invite should be all the instructions your guests will need to make it to the wedding. It's helpful to include the numbers and room prices of nearby hotels and contact details for reputable taxi firms that might come in handy. If you are having a long wedding weekend or an early morning wedding you may even want to include a list of local sights and attractions or restaurants for guests to visit the evening before the celebrations start. Some wedding guides suggest it's rude to include details of your gift list with the invitation and that guests will call to find out the details later on. This comes down to personal choice but consider whether you have ever attended a wedding where you've felt put out by being told where to find the gift list and perhaps canvass a number of close friends for their opinions. To most people it just makes common sense to include details; it saves the guests the trouble of calling and you guys the trouble of answering 150 calls about your gift list.

The gift list

Now this can be a fun job, although on paper it may not seem it. What other time in your life do you get to go into a department store and basically start pointing and saying 'I want one of those, and those and those'? It's a licence to choose all those things you've always wanted, and the only sticking point is your dearly beloved. She might not understand your need to own an original 1960s juke box or a full-sized pool table. You, on the other hand, might completely fail to grasp why she needs a set of casserole dishes that cost over £60 a piece. What exactly you do need will have to be decided between the two of you but the days when all you could have on your gift list were linens and crockery are long gone.

These days your gift list can include almost anything you want. All the major department stores will let you choose from most of their departments as well as including vouchers on your list to put towards larger items. A number of travel firms now let you set up your list with them and guests can put money towards your honeymoon or buy you treats to enjoy while you are away. Lots of smaller gift list companies will tailor your list to exactly what you need, whether you want to redo your garden, hire an interior designer, start a wine cellar or include experiences such as driving days and hot air balloon rides. And if you really have absolutely everything you could possibly need, a whole host of charities will happily take your guests' donations to sponsor needy children, trees, otters – you name it.

The only thing you might be frowned upon for requesting is cold hard cash. It might be exactly what you need but it's just not the done thing. If you have a particular thing that you want it to go towards, such as a deposit for your first house, perhaps include a note with the invite explaining this but make sure you have a small gift list somewhere too so that guests who really don't want to give you cash have another option.

Transport

The wedding day transport is a job that you and your best man should take charge of. It covers the following:

- the bridal car to take the bride and her father to the ceremony
- a car for the bridesmaids and the mother of the bride
- transport for you and the best man, if needed
- transport for you and the bride from the ceremony to the reception
- arranging a lift/taxi/hire car for heading off on your honeymoon.

You may also want to provide transport for some of your guests from the ceremony to the reception. Although this is by no means expected, an old London Routemaster bus, for example, will kick-start the party atmosphere and mean that guests can leave their cars behind for the rest of the day (see page 137 for where to hire one).

Dream machines

If you've ever dreamed of getting behind the wheel of a Ferrari or Bond's Aston Martin this could be the time to arrange it. Equally, if you've always had a thing about Del Boy's Robin Reliant or the A Team van, there are companies out there who can sort it out for you – whatever floats your boat. Just remember there's a certain class attached to turning up in an Aston Martin that won't be achieved in a Robin Reliant.

The cars for the bride and her maids are traditionally something classic such as a Rolls Royce but there are myriad different options, and if you both fancy something a bit more romantic or unconventional for getting to the reception perhaps consider one of the following:

- a horse and carriage
- a white London taxi
- a limo
- a pink Cadillac
- a sports car
- a helicopter
- a rickshaw
- a Hummer
- a white VW Beetle
- a trio of Minis, in the style of *The Italian Job*
- a motorcycle and side car (but not wise or safe for a bride with a really big dress)
- horseback
- a boat.

Before you book anything, think about the time of year you are getting married and how long a journey you'll need to make in the vehicle you choose. An open-top carriage is a bad idea for a winter wedding, while a lot of the older classic cars have a top speed of Very Slow, so are just not suitable for long journeys. If you opt for anything like a helicopter or boat obviously you will have to check a few things with your venue – landing space or a riverside location being the first to tick off on the checklist.

If budget is a real concern, think about borrowing a suitable car from a friend or using your own. Just make sure that you give the car a proper clean inside and out to make it feel a bit special and get a ribbon to go on the front. You don't want your bride making one of the most exciting journeys of her life surrounded by old crisp packets and empty Coke bottles.

The cake

The wedding cake is a traditional wedding essential that is usually cut and served after the wedding breakfast. If the picture in your mind is a frothy, high-rise confection, covered with iced flowers and little cherubs, relax. These days you can pretty much have whatever kind of cake you want. Tiered fruit cakes are still popular but if you don't like fruit cake there's nothing to stop you having chocolate cake or a sponge, or really going for it and having one tier of each. Alternatively, towers of individual cupcakes or *croquembouches* (a traditional French cake – a pyramid of cream-filled profiteroles covered in caramel and spun sugar) are becoming very popular. If you are on a tight budget, serve your cake instead of pudding. Just remember that some cakes, particularly fruit cakes, can take a long time to mature, so order yours with plenty of time to spare.

The wedding rings

This is another area that involves your money being removed from your pocket and placed in someone else's. And that's as it should be, because chances are you instigated this whole marriage thing by proposing so providing the wedding ring is entirely your own responsibility. This is something you can start shopping for fairly early on, or you may even have bought it at the same time as the engagement ring. If you want to have 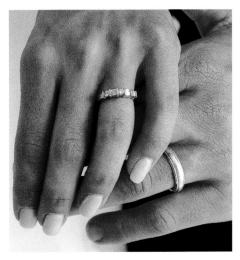 a ring made it can take at least a few months and even rings bought ready made may need to be resized, so plan at least a couple of months ahead.

The dress

This is the one task you are actually not allowed to be involved in. Traditionally the groom is not supposed to have any idea about what his bride will be wearing until she walks down the aisle as it's considered bad luck. Your bride might be relaxed about and let you know a few details but other than that it should all be big surprise for the wedding day.

Flowers

Your florist generally supplies the following:

- the bride's bouquet
- bouquets for the bridesmaids
- buttonholes and corsages
- table centrepieces
- any flower arrangements you would like to have at the ceremony.

As the groom you are traditionally responsible for paying for the bride's and bridesmaids' bouquets and the bridal party's buttonholes and corsages. This doesn't mean you are responsible for them full stop, as generally the bride will know what she wants for her and her attendants' bouquets – you might just be called on to supply some of the hard cash.

Buttonholes

Buttonholes for you and your attendants can be anything from a single rose in the wedding colours to more modern creations. A simple gerbera or orchid can look very effective. The groom usually has a slightly more elaborate buttonhole than the rest of his party and the flowers normally reflect those in the bride's bouquet.

Table centrepieces

Table centrepieces can range from a simple bowl of floating flower heads to towering creations in ornate vases dripping with orchids and trailing ivy. It basically comes down to your own personal style, the style of your venue and of course what your budget will allow. The basic rule for centrepieces is that they should be low enough for guests to talk over or high enough for guests to talk under. The atmosphere at your wedding will be severely curtailed if your guests can't see each other behind mountains of foliage.

Confetti

As you leave your ceremony it's traditional that guests pelt you with confetti of all shapes and sizes. Anything from the basic coloured paper horseshoe and bell shapes, to rice or dried rose petals is common today, you can even have personalised confetti with your picture stamped on it. Other modern alternatives also include bubbles, which the kids will love. Make sure you check with your church or venue as many would rather you didn't throw confetti on the premises because of the problem of cleaning it up, though you are more likely to be given the go-ahead if you can absolutely guarantee that only biodegradable confetti will be used.

Entertainment and music

Music and entertainment covers a variety of things. If you are having a religious ceremony you'll need to think about the songs you want played at various points in the ceremony and whether you'd like hymns to be sung. If you choose to have hymns a choir, even a very small one, is a good investment and will bolster the singing if your guests are on the quiet side. During the signing of the register it's popular to have some music, either from the church organist or from a vocal soloist or harpist to entertain your guests. At a civil ceremony, you might have a string quartet to accompany the entrance of the bride and the signing of the register or a CD of music chosen by you and the bride.

String quartets are also popular for the start of the reception when your guests are mingling with a glass of champagne, while something soothing like a gentle jazz band works well during the wedding breakfast. Alternatively, a CD of music that you've put together from your favourite tunes is another good option that will also save you money, or load up your iPod with dozens of good reception tunes and set it going so you won't have to worry about it for hours.

The first dance

You will need to choose a song for your first dance together after the wedding breakfast. You may already have a song that is 'your song', from when you first met, or your first date or that time sitting on a great beach together on your first holiday. That one will be perfect, as long as the words are suitable. It doesn't have to be a traditional slow dance – a funky dance number can be just as good.

If you don't have a particular song, spend some time going through your music collection to find something that speaks to you both. If you really can't find anything there are any number of romantic classics that will work perfectly well and hopefully sum up your feelings about each other. Again, just make sure you listen to the words: the sweetest, most delicate-sounding song can still have lyrics that are nothing to do with a loving couple and more to do with, say, gangsters in the Bronx.

It's a good idea to have a little practice dance at home to your chosen tune, particularly if it's a jazzy little number where you have the potential to really embarrass yourself. No one will expect you to perform amazing moves but if you did fancy learning to dance properly there are companies out there dedicated to choreographing couples for their first dance. They'll be able to teach you everything from a few simple pointers and a couple of basic moves to drop into your dance to choreographing you the whole thing complete with lifts and spins if you are feeling ambitious.

The evening entertainment

This is when you can get really creative. You may have seen the film *The Wedding Singer* and think you know what to expect, but wedding bands these days come in all shapes and sizes and are generally very good. Whatever your favourite style is you'll be able to find everything from cheesy Sixties and Seventies combos to Abba or Beatles tribute bands. For a slightly cheaper option, the classic wedding disco is still going strong and you are bound to have at least one relative who'll be desperate to strut their funky stuff as soon as the first riff from *The Birdie Song* comes on.

Most DJs are happy to be given a playlist of songs you would like to hear, so you should be able to tailor the music to your tastes. It's a nice idea to ask friends and family to email you their three favourite songs before the wedding and then pass this on to the DJ. That way everyone should get to hear something they like.

Entertainment doesn't just mean music either; in the modern world of weddings there's someone out there to cater for every whim you can think of.

How about:

- a caricaturist to draw guests during dinner
- a sleight of hand magician to mingle with the crowd at the drinks reception
- a clown or a bouncy castle for the kids
- fake guests or waiters who become more and more outrageous until they reveal they are performers
- a silhouette cutter
- contacting a fireworks company to arrange a display
- living statues? – yes, those guys who stand on the street pretending to be statues, they're available for weddings too
- casino tables for roulette and blackjack – particularly good if you are having an early ceremony and need something to fill the afternoon.

The seating plan

Now, this is a fairly big job that's a lot harder than it may initially seem. You are probably thinking: 'My friends and family are great. They all get on like a house on fire. There won't be any problems.' What will actually happen is that 10 of your 13 favourite university friends will fit on to one table and there'll be three stuck out on a limb somewhere else quietly fuming, while at the same time, cousin Joe – whom you previously thought was easy going – will be deeply upset that he's been placed at table six which he sees as way down the ranking from, say, table two where his brother is. Not to mention the hassle of seating people's children and the odd work colleague who doesn't know anyone.

Some couples opt to mix everyone up so everyone gets to know one another. If you go down this route try to include a couple of people on each table whom you know will liven up the conversation a little combined with maybe a few of your quieter friends. Others try to keep groups together, which can prove tricky if group numbers are bigger than your table sizes. If you have a fair few single friends it might be tempting to put them all together on a single's table. This can be a good idea but ensure there's a fairly even mix of men and women and try not to be too obvious about any matchmaking!

There are a few computer programs available to help you with the seating plan, such as the seating planner available at www.youandyourwedding.co.uk, where you can enter all your guests' names as well as noting perhaps exes who shouldn't sit together

and family members who don't get on. If you put them too close warning signs will start flashing. However, you don't need a computer program to help you if you apply a bit of common sense. Wherever people end up sitting, most of them will make the best of it – and realise it's not an indication of the strength of your relationship. If they don't then it's their problem. Realistically they will be sitting there for only a few hours at most so even the most socially inept guest should be able to deal with it – frankly there are a lot more important things for you to be thinking about.

You may also want to think about naming your tables as part of the decorations/theme. Good ideas include:

- places that have been important in your relationship
- countries you have visited
- using a picture from a different point in your lives on each table
- song titles
- football teams
- film titles
- romantic/funny quotes from films or books you both love.

There is a practical reason for this too as it means you can avoid offending people seated on table eight who think they should be on table one.

In addition to floral centrepieces (see page 73), you could choose to have favours and other items on the tables to delight and entertain your guests. See next page.

Decorating your venue

This can be a small or a massive job depending on the style of your venue and wedding. If you are marrying in a stately home, chances are your surroundings will already be fairly salubrious. Alternatively, a church hall or marquee may need a bit of extra work to liven it up. The co-ordinator at your wedding venue should be able to give you a few ideas, or flick through magazines for suggestions. If you are having a theme, kitting out your venue to match will be an important part of it.

Flowers always look beautiful but they can be very expensive, particularly if you are having a winter wedding. Save money by moving the flower displays – carefully! – from your ceremony to your reception and bulking out a few pretty flowers with foliage to make larger displays.

Favours

These are the little things you put on the table as gifts to your guests, regardless of the fact that you are giving them a whole day of free food, drink and entertainment. Traditionally a favour was a gift of five symbolic sugared almonds, but at a modern wedding favour boxes with gold-plated decorations are not unheard of and popular options include candles, chocolates, bars of soap and sweets wrapped in lurid pieces of frilly net. You are probably

thinking that they're no use to man nor beast. Your bride, on the other hand, is likely to be thinking: 'Ahh, what a cute little flowery favour box. That'll make a perfect gift that my guests will treasure forever, and they only cost £5 each!'

If you have money to spare what's the harm in indulging your guests? But if you are already having to tighten your belts then this is one thing you can do without – or do on the cheap. If your bride is getting carried away with expensive favours, remind her that only her mum will actually keep and treasure them forever and a good few of the others won't even get taken home from the reception.

The first night hotel

This is one hundred per cent your job and you need to get it right – messing up the first night of your married life together does not bode well. As more and more couples have lived together before the wedding, the traditional sight of newlyweds leaving the reception early and heading to a posh hotel for their first night of passion together, or even straight off on honeymoon, is becoming less and less common.

If you do plan to leave the reception early, get the best man to make sure your luggage is ready in the car. Try to find a nice hotel a short drive away from the reception and, if you are heading off on honeymoon the next day, pre-book a cab to the airport. Ideally find something that's a bit romantic and more luxurious than your normal standard.

A four-poster bed and an open fire never go amiss either. You can even add a few nice touches with perhaps a bottle of champagne or some chocolates and flowers for extra brownie points. Also make sure that you keep your destination a secret; arriving to find that your best man has got there first, filled your bed with confetti and sprayed 'Just Married' in shaving foam across the bathroom is guaranteed to take the gloss off your first night as man and wife.

If you plan to dance the night away and have no intention of leaving early it's polite to let guests know the plan. Some older guests will have been brought up to think that it's rude to leave the reception before the bride and groom so let them know if you don't expect them to follow this tradition.

If you are staying the night at your reception venue, you will probably have the bridal suite included as part of your package, thus saving you the trouble of organising something. Try to keep your room number a secret and tell the hotel not to give the key to anyone else, no matter how persuasive.

Wedding websites

Finally, if you want to avoid having to print out a hundred maps and so on, why not set up a wedding website? The bonus of this is you can put tons of information on a website that just won't fit in an envelope with your invites. Direct links to local hotels' websites, interactive maps, links to websites providing driving directions and local public transport information and even links to your gift list company are all a good idea. After the wedding you can then post your pictures online where guests from around the world can look at them. If you are IT-gifted, you could set up your own but there are also plenty of companies that will be expert at setting up and monitoring a site for you.

> ### SURVIVAL TIP 10
>
> *It's a good idea to have a quiet word with the bride about your wedding night and whether she's expecting a night of passion like never before or to fall into bed drunk at four o'clock in the morning and save it for the honeymoon. It's best to make sure you are both on the same wavelength; you don't want to be initiating a late night karaoke session at the reception while she wants to sneak away.*

8

The Stag Night

Forget the flowers, the cake and the bridesmaids' handbags.
Your biggest decision after deciding to get married is
what kind of stag night to have. When most grooms imagine
a traditional stag night it involves booze – lots of it – combined
with your best friends doing something unspeakably mean to you
such as tying you up naked in the street smeared in jam
or putting you on the Edinburgh sleeper train
with only your underpants for company.

A lot of this is merely urban myth. Have you ever actually been on a stag night where the groom ended up handcuffed to a lamppost? Although lots of stags would be a bit disappointed if their mates didn't do anything mean to them at all – it's how blokes show they care, after all – there are limits. And if all that sounds like your idea of hell, there are tons of other options for the less exhibitionist stag.

First things first. Have a word with your best man. Hopefully you will not have chosen a disorganised adrenalin-seeking booze-hound who loves making you do things you don't want to do. Ideally your best man will be someone who can organise a good party, will sort out a surprise or two but knows that he should draw the line at anything that might cause actual personal injury or the bride to cancel the wedding.

The plan

Officially you are not supposed to know too much about your own stag night but there's no harm in sitting down and talking through a few ideas and a few ground rules. Make sure you discuss the following:

- how much you want to spend
- whether you want to go abroad
- how many nights it should be
- a rough idea of numbers
- what kind of activities you would like
- what you will and won't be happy with – if you have a strong aversion to lap dancers, voice it now.

SURVIVAL TIP 11

On no account hold the stag night the evening before the wedding. This used to be the tradition but grooms have slowly realised that being hungover and smelling of beer on your wedding day, not to mention the chances of not making it to the wedding at all, is a really, really bad idea. Two to four weeks before the date is much more sensible – recovery time is essential.

Who to invite?

Start by making a list of all your close friends as well as work colleagues and close relatives. Don't feel you have to invite every single male friend you know. It should be mainly those with whom you have a long-standing and close relationship. Stag parties with more than twenty people can start to get a bit hard to organise, let alone control. It used to be traditional many, many moons ago, to invite both the bride's father and your father to the stag night. These days no one expects this. If you get on amazingly well with your father and your prospective father-in-law there's nothing to say you can't invite them, but it might strike the rest of the stags as odd. It may also not be the

most sensible idea to let the father-in-law see what you are like on a proper night out with the lads before you've persuaded his daughter to sign on the dotted line. If the bride has any brothers it's polite to invite them along, even if you don't know them very well. They'll be pleased to be invited and if they decide to come it will give you the opportunity to get to know them better.

A few good ideas…

There is a wealth of companies out there geared specifically to arranging a humdinger of a stag night for you. There is even one that's presently offering stag nights at the North Pole – for the price per person of a small car. You don't have to go quite that far to have a good time though although it's worth bearing in mind that there is nothing like a weekend away in a foreign country to persuade quieter friends to let their hair down a little and it's also great for getting all your mates bonding as a group.

Popular overseas destinations include:
- Amsterdam
- Barcelona
- Budapest
- Dublin
- Ibiza
- Prague.

Lots of companies offer a complete package, including hotel accommodation, entry into nightclubs and also an escort to help get you to the right place at the right time, which can be tricky in a foreign city.

Popular UK destinations include:
- Blackpool
- Brighton
- Dublin
- Edinburgh
- Liverpool
- London
- Newcastle
- Nottingham.

Daytime activities

The classic stag night activity is something like paintballing or go-karting, but in a competitive market stag night companies are falling over themselves to think of new and exciting ways to wear you out, for example you could try:
- Zorbing: you are strapped into a giant inflatable ball and then rolled down a hill, praying you are not going to be sick.

- Tank-driving: a chance to storm the fields of the nearest farmer, challenging all who get in your way. Some companies even offer tanks that fire paintballs – ingenious!
- Hovercraft racing: like your usual race but hovering an inch or so above the ground as if by magic.
- Human table football: if your normal five-a-side is a bit too energetic, try it strapped to a long pole – at least you won't have to run quite as far.
- Stuntman training: learn how to fall down a flight of stairs and leap out of open windows, although don't expect a movie career out of it.

Other less unusual activities that are proving popular include quad biking, white water rafting, golf, deep-sea fishing, five-a-side football, windsurfing and 4x4 driving. There's even a company offering stags the chance to fly a Mig jet. If there's something you've always wanted to try and you've got the money to spend, there's bound to be a stag night company who can sort it out for you. It probably won't be long before we see the first stag in orbit… although still with only his underpants and the bus fare home for company no doubt.

Evening activities

If you are not a drinking man you might think about the theatre, a comedy show or a nice restaurant and if you are a drinker then the world is your oyster. Before you decide on a bar or club, get your best man to call them first and if there's a guest list get you all on it. At the same time he should try to suss out their attitude towards stag parties as lots of places can be a bit sniffy, even if you are not expecting to be particularly rowdy. There's nothing worse than having nowhere to go at the end of the night so it's best to check first and make sure you are heading for somewhere that's happy to let you in.

Good ideas include:
- A night at the dogs: you can't beat greyhound racing for combining sport, beer and betting in one fell swoop.
- Horse racing: all the appeal of the dogs, just bigger animals and a bit more class.
- A party bus: lots of stag night companies offer a party bus service where you are ferried around town with plenty of drinks and given VIP entry into a number of different clubs.
- If you are on a budget, organising your own pub quiz: with a bit of effort on the best man's part this could be a real laugh. Find some space in your local or hire a

private room, work out some great questions, some good forfeits and a couple of prizes for the winners and a booby prize for the loser or groom.

- Love football? Head to Madrid for an afternoon watching Real Madrid play before a night on the town sampling the local tapas and vino.
- Just love sport in general? If there's any major sporting event – rugby, cricket, figure skating (maybe not!) – coming up it would make a great day out with your mates.
- Medieval jousting: it's a weird one but if you've always had a hankering for chain mail log on to www.knightsofmiddleengland.co.uk and get it booked up.
- Driving days: always a popular option, whether you go for budget friendly go-karting or racing a car of your choice on a proper circuit.
- If you and your friends are a little too suave and sophisticated for all this activity, why not start the afternoon at a male-friendly spa where you can enjoy a proper shave or a massage while drinking beers and watching sports on TV?
- If you like your drinks, think about doing an organised tour of a whisky distillery or visiting Vinopolis in London to taste a few fine wines.
- If you enjoy a game of golf, head to St Andrews in Scotland for a long weekend and combine a couple of rounds with a tour of a distillery and a night on the town.
- Head to a casino for a few hours. If that's a bit too pricey, set up some games at home and play for small change.

Just the two of us

Some couples opt for a joint hen and stag night and this is certainly an option if the traditional rowdy hen and stag party is just not the thing for either of you. Hiring a private room in a restaurant for you and a few friends is a great option or maybe even taking over a country house for a weekend where both parties can do separate activities in the daytime before getting back together in the evening.

Money, money, money

However much the stag night is going to cost, it's the best man's responsibility to make everyone aware of it. Don't be upset if you are opting for something a bit lavish and some friends say they can't afford it; you can't force anyone to come or spend more than they want to. When it comes down to what you pay, some groups will club together to pay for the groom's share while others may expect you to foot the bill for the meal or the first round of drinks. If you are going away for an expensive weekend, don't expect your costs to be covered, although hopefully your mates will at least get in a few rounds of drinks for you.

Surviving your stag night

- Make sure you head out with plenty of money and a fully charged phone. They may both be taken away from you at some point in the evening but it's worth a try.
- Try to sneak in a few glasses of water between the comedy drinks they're probably going to make you drink. If he tries to stop you, remind your best man that he's supposed to be showing you a good time – not putting you in A&E to have your stomach pumped.
- If your mates bring something for you to wear that's less than flattering then summon your courage, be a sport and wear it... unless it's likely to get you arrested.
- Whatever you end up doing and wherever you end up, make sure you are within reach of a couple of paracetamol and a good greasy fry-up the following morning. They will both do you the world of good.
- When your bride innocently asks afterwards about the stag night don't tell her too much. If it wasn't debauched enough she'll lose all respect for you and if it was she'll hurt you, regardless of how debauched her hen night was.

9

The Speech

There's not nearly so much pressure on you as there
is on your best man so try to relax. Just imagining how he must feel
leading up to the most anticipated speech of the night should be
enough to calm your nerves. There are only a few things that are
really expected from the groom's speech and they're quite easily
achievable, no matter how bad a public speaker you are.

Traditionally the father of the bride speaks first and thanks all the guests for coming. He then normally says a few words about his daughter before proposing a toast to the happy couple. After he's sat down it's your turn. Your major jobs are:

- to thank the father of the bride for his speech and his toast
- to say something about how happy you are today and something about your fantastic new wife
- to give out thank-you gifts to your best man and ushers, as well as the bridesmaids, the mothers of the bride and groom and anyone else who may have helped out – your neighbour who made the cake for example
- to finish by toasting the bridesmaids.

Your speech is then followed by the best man's. His role is to thank you for your toast to the bridesmaids, on their behalf, and also to offer thanks from any other attendants. After that he's expected to launch into a humorous speech with plenty of anecdotes about you but finding a tone that will appeal to both your lewdest mates and your grandma, plus he has to manage not to offend anyone whilst still being entertaining. Finally he has to say something nice about you too before proposing a toast to the happy couple. It's a tall order.

It's not unusual these days for the chief bridesmaid to stand up to say a few words. The best man speech is always the one most anticipated so it's generally saved until last so, while the chief bridesmaid can be fitted into the order wherever seems most appropriate, perhaps the best choice is just before the best man.

There are a few basic rules that you would do well to adhere to:

- You need to be entertaining but, more importantly, sincere. Your guests will be expecting the best man to provide the belly laughs not you, so they will really just want to hear something about how important this day and your new wife are to you.
- Try not to get carried away. Any more than seven minutes is really too long.
- Commit as much of your speech to memory as you can so that you can look at your guests or your bride when you are speaking. If you can't do that, at least memorise the opening lines and then try to look up as much as possible when you are reading from your sheet.
- Speak loudly and try not to rush. The temptation will be to speed through it all if you are nervous but it will come across as garbled. Guests won't know what you are saying and therefore you won't get the responses you are after.

Don't go it alone

It's not unusual these days for your bride to want to stand up and say a few words too. There's no traditional format for when and how she does this so it's really up to you both. She might want to follow you, before the best man has a turn, or it might be nice if she speaks directly after her father and personally thanks him for his kind words about her. Equally, you could stand up together and share a speech, which means she can also take part in giving out thank-you gifts and take some of the pressure off you.

Just a shy guy

If the thought of standing up in front of a crowd is giving you sleepless nights, try to stay calm. If you are being made deeply unhappy by the whole idea, then you don't have to say any more than the minimum thank yous and toasts. But remember that this is a one-off moment in you life, so it might be a shame to let it pass without saying something. Everyone at the wedding will want the best for you; they are your friends and it is your wedding day, so they're really not going to be mean.

Top tips for overcoming nerves

- Practise, practise, practise. It's boring but practice really does make perfect and it will make you feel more confident if the words just roll off your tongue.
- Have a glass of water on stand-by in case your mouth goes dry.
- Make sure you take a few deep breaths before standing up and focus on breathing properly throughout the speech. It will make your delivery better, ensuring you speak slowly and clearly, and help to calm you down.

The Speech

> ### SURVIVAL TIP 12
>
> *If you know you have a few cheeky friends who might heckle during your speech, have a couple of witty retorts ready and everyone will be astounded by your seemingly off-the-cuff comebacks.*

- Put key phrases on to cue cards. Some speakers like to write their words out verbatim but this may lead to you hiding behind the paper and never looking up. Cue cards will simply remind you of the main points in case you forget them. Also, if you are nervous, paper can flap around a bit while cue cards should stay steadier.
- Project your voice so you sound confident, even if you are not feeling it. Practise this at home in front of your bride-to-be or a good friend.
- Have a glass or two of Dutch courage – but not too many. You will certainly embarrass yourself if you try to deliver your speech when drunk and it will be caught on someone's camera for all time. Just picture the clips of drunken bridegrooms and best men on those video-funnies television programmes if you feel yourself reaching for a third drink.
- Make a good impression as you stand up by allowing your arms to hang naturally and keeping your body straight. An easy relaxed bearing will make you feel better and look more confident.
- Try and smile as you give your speech. It's easy to look stern faced when you're nervous.
- If you are feeling really nervous try to look just at the table closest to you so you don't feel overwhelmed by the numbers of people.
- Finally, smile and remember that the best man probably feels a lot more nervous than you do right now, which should pay him back for anything mean he did to you on the stag night.

10

The Stress Factor

If you look through the nearest wedding guidebook
or magazine – and being in close proximity to a bride-to-be there's
likely to be several hundred within easy reach – you'll see hundreds of
smiley faces: pictures of happy couples choosing their gift list items;
jubilant brides and bridesmaids looking at sparkly jewellery;
and positively ecstatic mothers of the bride sharing jokes with
their future sons-in-law. This may lull you into a false sense
of security and into thinking that wedding planning
is all hearts and flowers – it's not.

For your own safety, and so you can recognise the telltale signs, the unofficial dictionary definition of Bridezilla is as follows:

Bridezilla n.: a woman who, in the run-up to her wedding day, has taken on some of the frightening characteristics of Godzilla, creature of the deep, in her quest for the perfect big day. Known by the mad-eyed, unblinking stare caused by spending too many hours sticking together diamanté-encrusted wedding invitations, and her crazed roaring when confronted with a delivery of the wrong colour napkin rings, her defining characteristic is a total lack of control or reason where her wedding day is concerned.

You may find that, having popped the question, you've opened up yourself and your partner to some of the worst arguments you've ever had. Unless you are one of those couples who agree on absolutely everything or you are a groom who really doesn't care as long as his bride likes it (although this can be a source of stress in itself) there are likely to be a few humdingers.

Don't panic! It doesn't mean you should call the whole thing off; it's fairly normal. When else in your lives will you have to throw the biggest party you've ever thrown, catering for all your nearest and dearest in one room and spending a huge amount of money doing it? When else will you care quite so much about the sun shining or your four-year-old nephew having spilled ketchup on his outfit? For what other occasion in her life will your bride start planning her hair, make-up and skincare regime six months in advance and start a diet so strict that it mainly comprises lettuce, with cabbage as an occasional treat?

SURVIVAL TIP 13

If you really aren't interested in the colour of the bridesmaids' shoes and it causes friction, try to reassure your bride that it doesn't mean you are not interested in her or the wedding. It simply means satin-heeled court shoes aren't your thing!

Get it in perspective

The only answer is for both of you to try to take a step back now and again. Depending on how deeply embedded you bride is in the World of Weddings, she may not want to hear this from you, but try to remind her that her big day doesn't need to look exactly like a glossy magazine wedding, and chances are it won't. Things may not go entirely to plan, the photographer you want may be booked up or your favourite band simply too expensive – they are not important in the grand scheme of things. You also both need to remind yourselves why you started all this in the first place, and whether your argument about how big the centrepieces should be or whether Aunty Joan should sit on the same table as Uncle Bob really matters that much. Don't forget, the most important part of the day is generally the cheapest and easiest bit to organise – the part when the two of you say your vows.

Dealing with stress

- Delegate, delegate, delegate. If your bride is feeling a bit overwhelmed and has started to develop a nervous twitch when she hears the word 'wedding', help her. Offer to take on a few more roles and show her just what a great husband you are going to make, while at the same time making your life a hell of a lot easier. Weigh up the hassle of a few hours on the internet and a few phone calls compared to a steaming row every other week and walking on eggshells the rest of the time.
- If you are both struggling under the pressure, ask family and friends to help; they'll usually be more than keen. Ask one of your mothers to manage the RSVP list while the other one co-ordinates the flowers. Perhaps your dad could help out with the entertainment? Get your bride's friends round for the evening to help write the placecards or make the invitations or favours. Ply them with some food and drink and they'll be happy to help.
- If it's really all becoming too much, invest in a wedding co-ordinator to oversee everything and make sure the day runs to plan. It will cost you a bit extra but, if it helps you both to de-stress and keeps you happy and on the path to marriage, it will be money well spent.

Once you've delegated, you can then start to spend your new free time doing the following to ward off the onset of more Bridezilla (and Groomzilla? You never know…) behaviour:

- Eat to beat stress – apparently eating a load of the right food, such as fresh fruit and vegetables and plenty of wholefoods, can help combat stress. Cutting down on salt, sugar and processed foods as well as stimulants such as tea, coffee and alcohol should also help.
- If this doesn't sound like much fun, and as far as you're concerned giving up your morning cuppa will do you more harm than good, try eating to beat stress by taking your strung-out beloved to a fancy restaurant on a proper date and agreeing to not talk about weddings at all. Add a few nice glasses of wine into the equation and you should both be suitably happy.
- If a date's just not enough, how about a long weekend away, wedding talk not allowed? Remind yourselves why you are getting married in the first place.
- A bit of exercise is also a good way to take yourself away from the wedding planning for a bit of personal time, not to mention being a mood-enhancer itself.
- Get plenty of sleep. Easier said than done sometimes but give it a go.
- Surprise your fiancée by booking her in for a massage or a facial. She'll love it. Alternatively, give her a foot rub yourself – she'll be putty in your hands.
- Both of you need to learn how to say no. There will be people who want to have a say in how you have your wedding day but it's your day and, while you should listen to people's suggestions, you also have every right to politely turn them down or tell them that you prefer to do things a different way.

Pre-wedding nerves

If your stress is being caused by something more than just the colour of the tablecloths or whether to wear a waistcoat and you are having a bout of the pre-wedding jitters, try not to worry. It is quite normal for both partners to feel a bit daunted and question what they are doing at some point during the engagement, particularly after a few deposits have

SURVIVAL TIP 14

If all your efforts to calm her down and reassure her are falling on deaf ears, point her in the direction of the chat rooms at www.youandyourwedding.co.uk. She'll be able to share the horror of failing to source the right kind of chocolate fountain with people who truly understand her – other brides-to-be.

been put down and money has been spent. Getting married is a big thing and shouldn't be taken lightly – it's human nature to be a little uncertain. It would probably be more unusual for you not to be a little bit scared!

If your jitters last more than a few weeks and start to become something serious, that's the time to worry. Tell your partner how you feel and consider putting the wedding back a little if need be, particularly if other important life events have happened – such as the loss of a loved one – to give you time to resolve any problems.

SURVIVAL TIP 15

If you can feel a pre-wedding slanging match brewing, go for a quick walk. Walk round the block to cool off and then head home to resume discussing whatever it is calmly.

Parental control

Rowing with your partner may be the least of your worries and it may be her or your parents who are causing the arguments. If either set of parents is contributing towards the wedding they may feel they can have some say in the arrangements. It's polite to listen to what they think but if it's something you really don't want or aren't happy with then there is nothing wrong with putting your foot down. It is your day after all.

Little white lies

It may be very tempting to tell the odd little white lie, such as 'the bridesmaids headdresses look great' or 'no darling, I'm totally happy to stand in a receiving line', to protect yourself from the horror of any more wedding planning stress. Tread carefully; if you couldn't give two hoots about the bridesmaids' headdresses and your bride's happy then fair enough. If you're actually going to be quietly fuming about standing in line and greeting your guests for an hour and a half, then be honest. You don't want to be forced to do anything you don't want to on the big day and it's certainly not a great way to start a relationship by lying, no matter how well intentioned.

11

The Honeymoon

Just imagine it: the planning is all over and your wedding day
has passed in a happy blur of love, good feeling and a fair bit of food
and drink. Now it's just you and your fabulous new wife dipping
your toes in the blue sea and drinking
tequila sunrises on a beach somewhere.
This is one of those jobs that even
the most lacklustre groom
should enjoy sorting out.

Traditionally it is the groom's responsibility to book and pay for the honeymoon. Lots of brides still love their honeymoon to be a total surprise but equally your bride-to-be might want a say in where she's going, just as you might want her to contribute more than just her opinions. However you arrange it, this should be a really pleasurable job.

The world is your oyster. Top honeymoon destinations include:

- The Bahamas
- The Caribbean
- Fiji (or elsewhere in the South Pacific)
- The Maldives
- Mauritius
- New York
- Paris
- Scotland
- Thailand
- Venice.

Decide on your budget first. If it will just about stretch to the Caribbean but when you get there you won't be able to afford more than a one-star hovel in a dodgy backwater, why not head to Scotland or France instead, where you can spend all that spare airfare on really plush five-star accommodation and some great treats? Just be a bit creative with your cash.

Booking tips

You may have a good idea of your wedding date well in advance and also exactly when you want to head off on honeymoon, in which case you may be able to take advantage of early booking offers and discounts. If you book really early you may even be able to specify things such as seats and rooms. Another way to save money – particularly if you are having a Saturday wedding – is to wait a few days before you travel, as weekend flights can be more expensive. This will also give you a bit of time to recover after the wedding and sort out your luggage.

Find a good tour operator to help you and suggest different options, and pick up plenty of brochures and wedding magazines for ideas. If your bride wants a surprise honeymoon but you have no idea where to take her, get some help. Ask her friends and family for ideas and to ask her a few subtle questions. Some tour operators will even liaise between the two of you and speak to her about what she'd like before coming back to you for a final decision and to book the holiday. That way they can steer you in the right direction for her dream trip.

Two-centre honeymoons

If one just isn't enough, two-centre honeymoons are a great way of combining two different types of destinations. If you like the idea of visiting a big city but also know you will need a bit of relaxation time after the wedding, perhaps combine a few days in a bustling city like New York with a week on a beach in Hawaii. Or think about combining a week on safari with a week in a luxury hotel in Cape Town. If the two of you have quite different interests, make sure you accommodate them both – for example a hotel with a golf course for you and a spa and a nearby city for her.

Unusual escapes

There is nothing to say that just because it's your honeymoon you have to go for the traditional option of two weeks on a beach. If the idea bores you both ridged there are plenty of other alternatives:

- Book into Sweden's Ice Hotel for plenty of cosy nights under warm blankets. Just remember to pack your thermal underwear.
- If you are both active, head to the slopes for a skiing or snowboarding holiday.
- If the budget is tight, buy a camper van and tour round Europe (don't surprise the missus with this one just in case she's expecting something more lavish).
- Head to Vegas for a roller coaster trip of sights, sounds, gambling and... well... roller coasters!
- During the winter months try Reykjavik, Iceland where you may catch a glimpse of the northern lights.
- Have the world's best diving experience on Australia's Great Barrier Reef.

Be prepared

Wherever you end up going, make sure you've checked what inoculations you may need before you fly. Your travel agent should be able to tell you. If you are unsure, have a look at the British Airways Travel Clinic website (see page 134) or www.netdoctor.com. It's also worth checking the Foreign Office website (see page 134) if you are going somewhere off the beaten track to be certain it's safe to travel there.

Honeymoon checklist

Along with a vat of sun cream and far too many clothes for just seven days, make sure you take the following:

- ✓ valid 10-year passports: some countries won't accept passports that have less than six months left on them
- ✓ travel insurance
- ✓ local currency, including a few small notes for taxi drivers and tips on arrival
- ✓ a first-aid kit with basics such as insect repellent, paracetamol, plasters and so on.

What's in a name?

If your bride is changing her name you will need to plan this into your honeymoon departure date. Things can get complicated, particularly in this climate of heightened security, and if the name on her boarding pass and passport don't match up it's unlikely you'll be able to get on the plane. It may be simpler to book everything in her maiden name and sort out changing documents once you are back from the honeymoon.

Freebies

Is it actually possible to get upgraded to first class and plied with free champagne just because you are newlyweds? Frankly, it's worth a try and if you don't ask you definitely won't get. Make it clear to your tour operator at the time of booking that this is your honeymoon and also mention it to the reception staff when you get to your hotel. Arrive early at the airport, making sure you are looking presentable, and you never know your luck. If you are a bit shy about telling your hotel you are honeymooners, get someone in your family or a friend to call up and have a word with them as a 'surprise' for you. If you don't want the stress of trying to wangle a free upgrade you can often pay a little extra simply to use the Business Class lounges of most airlines, which should guarantee you slightly more luxurious surroundings while you wait for your flight.

The Big Day – the Ceremony

Right, the big day is about to dawn and hopefully you are bang up to speed with your outfit, all the jobs that have been entrusted to you (including putting the final flourishes on your speech), and the wedding in general. Ideally you will have survived the stag night with no major injuries or indiscretions and you and your betrothed are still on speaking terms.

The week before…

There may be a few minor jobs left over for you to do this week, such as picking up any hire suits with your best man and checking that all the ushers know where they're supposed to be and when – although try to let the best man do most of the worrying about that. There may also be the question of where you stay the night before the wedding. If you are living together, your fiancée may want to get ready there, in which case you'll need to stay with your best man. Alternatively, she may want to stay at her family home if it's nearby, which means you can have the run of the house. It's traditional for the bride and groom not to see each other the night before the wedding and in the morning before the ceremony as it's supposed to be bad luck. If you are not particularly superstitious, don't feel you have to stay apart but bear in mind that it's a special moment when you turn round and see your bride in all her finery for the first time at the start of the ceremony.

The rehearsal

It's standard procedure to have your rehearsal the night before the wedding – or as close to then as possible – and get together all the main players such as the bridesmaids, your best man, the father of the bride, possibly any young attendants and obviously yourselves. It's generally

SURVIVAL TIP 17

This is the last week of your single lives together. However much else is going on, make time for a last date together as girlfriend and boyfriend.

not necessary for all your ushers to attend as the best man can fill them in on what they need to do on the morning of the wedding. At the rehearsal you can practise what you'll be saying, how the music will come in, how the bride will walk up the aisle and how you'll both walk down it together. For a church wedding, the officiant will generally be there to go through your lines. For a civil ceremony you may want to have a rehearsal at the venue to plan the bride's entrance and the music but it's not usual for the registrar to be there as well, as you will have already checked your vows and readings with them at an earlier meeting.

In the USA it's common for the bride and groom to hold a rehearsal dinner the night before that's almost as lavish as the wedding breakfast itself, but the British tend to be a wee bit more understated. Following the rehearsal it's quite nice – but not expected – to all head out for a final meal together somewhere nearby and a low-key meal at an informal restaurant is perfectly good.

Just you and your mates…

With your bride probably packed off to her parents you have quite a long night stretching out in front of you. You may have your ushers and your best man staying with you or just your best man. Whether you are alone or in company, it may be tempting to help the hours pass and calm the nerves with a few drinks. This is a perfectly sensible idea and probably how you normally fill your time with your mates but try to be restrained.

It's a hard thing to have to say to your mates that enough's enough but this is the one night when you really do have to do it. They may give you a rough time but stick to your guns. Tonight your loyalty is to your bride and the promises you will make to her in the morning. If you make them hungover and smelling of last night's beer it suggests you are not really giving them your best shot. Perhaps think of a few diversionary tactics, rent a film, play a few card games or cook a slap-up meal between you to occupy the time. At least make sure you have a few glasses of water to give yourself a fighting chance.

Thank you and good night

Head to bed at a reasonable hour so that you can curtail any drinking and have a go at getting at least a few hours' shut-eye. Chances are you'll be a bit too nervous to get a proper night's sleep but it's worth giving it a try. Make sure both you and your best man have an alarm set, ideally two each, with one set for 10 minutes later in case you go back to sleep.

It's all in the timing

If you are having a fairly early wedding there may well be no time to do anything other than shower, get dressed and then head out. If your wedding isn't until mid- to late afternoon then you'll have a couple of hours to kill. Assuming that most guys won't take quite as long as their bride to get ready, you might want to think of something nice to do during the morning that will take your mind off the impending nuptials:

- book in for an early round of golf
- hire a couple of films
- go to a professional barber and get a wet shave
- if you normally enjoy a morning run or swim, there's no reason why you can't do this to calm your nerves a little.

If you don't have quite enough time to indulge in an activity make sure you have as long a lie-in as your nerves will allow, have an extra-long bath or shower, scrub your fingernails and take your time shaving – partly so you look great but also so you feel really relaxed. The most important thing to do in the morning, even if you don't do anything else, is have a hearty breakfast. A good, bulky fry-up is just what the doctor ordered or at least a few rounds of toast and a bowl of cereal. Breakfast will help to settle your stomach and it might be a good few hours before you sit down to your wedding breakfast.

SURVIVAL TIP 18

Call your bride. You are not supposed to see her the morning of the wedding but there is no rule against talking to her. Give her a call, check she's OK and tell her how much you are looking forward to later.

Put together a small bag of things to take with you to cover most emergencies, which can be left in the car at the ceremony. It should include the following:

- deodorant
- mints
- lip balm
- aftershave
- a change of clothes for the next day
- emergency cash
- your speech notes
- thank-you gifts
- car/house keys.

And don't forget your buttonhole! Or that it goes on the left lapel.

Let's go

Aim to arrive at the venue at least half to three-quarters of an hour before the ceremony is due to start. If you are at all worried about traffic then leave even earlier and if there are no hold-ups you have a chance to find a nearby pub and have a (small!) glass of Dutch courage. Your best man should have called the ushers during the morning to check they were all okay on time for getting to the church. It's their job to hand out the orders of service and greet all the guests. If you have the time and inclination, you can greet guests too, but don't feel you have to if it might make you nervous.

As the guests arrive, keep an eye on how the venue is filling up. If people are sitting towards the back, suggest that a few move forward to fill up the space evenly, or ask the ushers to do this.

Five minutes before the bride is due to arrive, you and the best man should take your places at the front.

Final thoughts

This is it – the moment that all this has been leading up to!

- Take a few deep breaths and don't think about everyone behind you. Just think about your beautiful bride.

- Remember to say your vows slowly and clearly, with as much volume as you can manage – although don't bellow them.

- Try to look into your bride's eyes as you say your vows and enjoy yourself.

SURVIVAL TIP 19

Check the best man has the rings – it's a stereotype but just occasionally the best man does actually misplace the rings. Don't let this happen to you.

- You may think it'll be your bride who'll get a little tearful but tons of grooms get caught out by their emotions when it comes to the crunch. If you find yourself welling up, don't try to speak through the tears. The officiant will allow you a little time to compose yourself.

- At a religious ceremony, once you are officially husband and wife you proceed to the vestry to sign the register with your wife on your left arm. Once you are ready to leave the church you again give her your left arm.

- Make sure that before the ceremony you have a quick think about how you're going to 'kiss the bride'. It needs to have passion but not so much that your nan feels faint.

- Finally, remember to slip a tissue into your pocket just in case either of you need it. This is your last responsibility as a fiancé as it's an unusual wedding dress that has a pocket for a hanky!

The Big Day –
the Reception

Once the vows have been said, you and your new wife sign the register before leaving your ceremony to anything from a peal of bells to the Wedding March to Meat Loaf. Whatever it is, it signifies the end of the serious part of the day and the start of the celebrations.

Your main responsibilities of getting yourself dressed and to the venue on time have all finished, and now it's just left for you to mingle with your guests, look happy and let them congratulate you. After the ceremony, traditionally couples have a few formal photographs taken before getting into the wedding car to be driven to the reception venue. This ride is a great time to spend a few minutes alone with your new wife, share a glass of champagne and take some time to think about the fact that you've just got married. This may well be the only time you spend alone together for the rest of the afternoon so make the most of it. If it's only a short drive, get the driver to take you round the block a few times.

If your ceremony and reception are being held in the same place, ask the venue staff beforehand if there is a quiet room where you can have a couple of minutes together immediately after the ceremony. You won't need to mingle with your guests straight away.

The receiving line

One decision that needs to be made before the day is whether to have a receiving line.

Pros:

- You'll get to see everyone who was at the ceremony and let them congratulate you. If you don't do it then there is a chance you'll be so busy later on that some people will inadvertently get missed out.
- Your parents and attendants will get a chance to meet everyone you've invited and put names to faces.
- Guests will be able to congratulate you personally as well as both sets of parents.

Cons:

- Have you ever shaken hands with 150 people? Imagine you spend just 30 seconds saying hello to each person; it will still take you over an hour to get through the lot.
- A lot of guests won't be happy to just say congratulations. They'll want to stop and chat, dramatically increasing the time it takes and making everyone at the back very impatient.
- Repetitive strain injury, not just to your arm – think about the number of times you'll have to say, 'Thank you so much, yes we're very happy'.

It's traditional to have the married couple, both sets of parents and also the best man and chief bridesmaid in the receiving line but you can cut down how long it takes by leaving out the parents and the attendants and just having the two of you greeting guests. If you decide to skip the receiving line altogether, make a point of getting up during the meal and wandering round to each table as a couple just to say hello to everyone and to let them congratulate you.

Mingling with the crowd

This may be the only time when all your friends, family and work colleagues will be together in one room. It is also probably the only time when you will be in a room with a hundred-odd people that you know. The only problem you might have with socialising will be that so many people will want a piece of you. Don't feel you have to stay and talk to one person for any length of time and don't feel embarrassed to excuse yourself to circulate a little. The only person you need to make sure you spend plenty of time with is your new bride. Try to do a bit of mingling together so you get to chat and experience the day as a couple.

Make time to eat

You may be feeling a bit nervous before your speech but try to make sure you eat some of the wedding breakfast that you are paying a lot of money for. It will help to stop you from passing out on the dance floor and also ensure you don't get completely sozzled. There's absolutely nothing wrong with getting nicely merry to celebrate your own wedding day but do try to make sure you don't end up passed out in a broom cupboard before you and your bride make the first cut in the wedding cake.

The first dance

After your speech the only other thing you have to do is not tread on your bride's toes during the first dance. Depending on how happy you are on a dance floor, your first dance can be a romantic slow dance with your beloved or a gut-wrenchingly embarrassing moment when you are forced to dance in front of all your friends and relatives without the protection of having had eight pints of strong lager. See page 74 for how to choose the right song – and making your feet do what you want them to.

When to wrap it up

If you are planning to leave the reception before your guests to head off to your first night hotel then everything will come to a natural end. Most venues will have a cut-off point when the music has to finish, so forty minutes to an hour before that would be a good time to leave. If you are being ultra-traditional you will both disappear to change into your leaving outfits. Your attendants should assemble all the guests outside so they can wave you off in your post-wedding transport – probably a perfectly lovely car that at some point in the evening will have been horribly defaced with shaving foam and tin cans. If your best man is particularly inventive, best check under the bonnet for bits of old fish.

The Big Day – the Reception

> ### SURVIVAL TIP 20
>
> *Make sure neither of you spends the last hour of your reception apologising to guests for not being able to speak to them enough during the day – nobody will mind.*

Some venues do not have a licence past a certain time so that will also bring a natural end to your reception. If it is in a hotel, often the main party will have to finish at midnight but guests staying in the hotel will be able to retire to the hotel bar for a nightcap. If you and your bride plan to stay up late, ask your hotel about providing something like bacon butties for late night revellers; they will go down a storm.

The morning after…

With the huge number of hotels now licensed for weddings, it's become more common for newlyweds to stay the night at their venue and to reconvene with their guests the morning after over a hearty breakfast. This can provide quite a nice end to the weekend and is a great time for chatting about the day before. Alternatively, if you'd rather be alone together the morning after your wedding, consider booking your first night at a different hotel from your guests.

Final things to tidy up

While you are away there will be a few final things that need to be sorted out:

- Make sure someone is in charge of returning all the hire outfits as they generally need to be back the first working day after the wedding.
- If you've had single-use cameras on the tables, ask someone to be responsible for collecting them at the end of the night. Most come with developing costs pre-paid so, to save time, get the same person to send them off to be developed while you are away. Pick them up yourselves when you get back so you are the first people to see them.
- Ask your best man and maid of honour to check that everything is tidied up at the end of the reception and to ensure that anything that was hired for the table decorations, catering etc. will be returned while you are away.
- Get someone to collect up any flower arrangements you want to keep and organise their transport or offer them to guests who might want to take them home.
- If there are any outstanding bills to settle such as a bar bill or the band's fee ask the best man to sort them out on your behalf and reimburse him later.

And remember…

It is very likely that something on your wedding day won't go exactly to plan. One of the ushers may not have the right waistcoat, the weather may be bad or the band may hit traffic and turn up late. This may upset your bride more than you or you may both feel a bit annoyed after all that planning. Try to remember that none of the guests knows what cufflinks you were meant to be wearing or that the flower girl has the wrong shoes on. All they care about is seeing both of you having a great time. If the weather doesn't look promising your venue will have a contingency plan and sort it out so don't stress, and try to stop your bride from getting stressed too. If you both keep calm and simply focus on enjoying the day together then nothing else will really matter.

14

The End?

Of course it's not the end. It may be the end of your big day and nearly the end of this book but, as for your lives together, this has just been a big party to mark the beginning of hopefully an amazing and long-lasting marriage.

It is not uncommon, after spending the best part of a year building up to the big day and then the honeymoon, to come back to earth afterwards with a bit of a bump. Following the honeymoon, try to make your first few days back at home a bit special with maybe a meal out or an overnight stay in a nice hotel. You could perhaps even arrange for a friend or parent to drop in just before you get home to fill up your fridge with milk and bread along with a few treats to make it all a bit more palatable.

Feeling gifted

You will still have the fun of opening all the presents from your gift list, which is like a really fantastic Christmas where absolutely everyone actually bought you something you want. Unfortunately, as is always the way, this must be followed by the slightly trickier job of remembering who got you what and then sending out the appropriate thank-you cards. It is nice to put a personal message in each one, mentioning the gift and how much you like it, no matter how time consuming it might be. Try to do it as soon as you can after you get back from your honeymoon – if you are doing this nearer to your first anniversary than your wedding day then you have left it far too late!

Photographs

The other wedding reminder you will have is your photographs. Most photographers will try to have them ready for you for when you get back from your honeymoon. Depending on what kind of package you have gone for, you will probably be given a selection of proofs to choose your final number from. Take time over your selection and let friends and family have a look too. If you had cameras on your table you should get plenty of your own pictures from them. Chances are that most of them will be a bit ropey but it will have been worth it for the one or two gems from each camera and will at least ensure that you have a picture of practically everyone who attended the wedding even if your photographer didn't catch them.

So there you are… married

Everything will probably all feel a bit new for a while and you will definitely spend a lot of time fiddling with your wedding band until you get used to wearing it. Apart from the shiny new ring on your finger, though, how much will have changed? These days a huge number of couples already live together before they marry, sharing living costs and most of the details of their lives. For example, it is unlikely that your wedding night will be when you first find out what side of the bed she prefers to sleep on. Neither of you should expect any dramatic changes just because you've become husband and wife – you are both still exactly the same people. You have made a huge commitment to keep doing the same things you were doing already – it's just that it's for the rest of your lives.

If anyone knew what the secret was to having a happy marriage he or she would probably be relaxing in a palatial mansion in Barbados and getting rich on the proceeds. One thing that is certain is that it takes a lot of work, and the phrase 'for better or worse' is included in your vows for a reason. Simple things, such as still making time to do all the nice things that you did when you were boyfriend and girlfriend, are worth their weight in gold. Just because your girlfriend has suddenly become a wife doesn't mean that she has stopped enjoying going out on romantic dates, spending time with you or having long weekends away. It also doesn't mean getting so comfortable together that you take each other for granted. Each day both of you should make that little bit of effort to be helpful and considerate of the other person's feelings and, most importantly, to say 'I love you'.

And finally…

There, that's it. The whole road from engagement to marriage mapped out for you, with a few tips on your future lives together thrown in for free. Hopefully you will have finished this with a better idea of what's required of you on your wedding day and the realisation that planning your wedding needn't be the bride's exclusive domain. It may even have dawned on you that there are some bits you could actively enjoy. And even if all you've learned is how to calm down a frenzied Bridezilla, high on sugared almonds, by persuading her to put down her wedding file, taking her out for dinner and pretending you know about table decorations and satin shoes then it has all been worthwhile.

Most importantly, just make sure you enjoy your wedding day and the run up to it. Being engaged should be a great time in both your lives. After all, you are planning a giant party especially to celebrate how happy you are and how much you are in love. Regardless of how much or how little you want to be involved, try to put your own stamp on the day. It's not all about the bride; it's about both of you creating your perfect day together – and promising to stay together for the rest of your lives.

Just one final survival tip from the worldly wise Ogden Nash on keeping your marriage on the right track. It is sound advice …

> ### SURVIVAL TIP 21
>
> *To keep your marriage brimming*
> *With love in the loving cup,*
> *Whenever you are wrong, admit it,*
> *Whenever you are right, shut up.*
> Ogden Nash, *A Word To Husbands*

15

Your Countdown to the Big Day

The following is your countdown to the wedding, with handy boxes to tick off along the way when each task is completed. Not everyone is going to have 12 months in which to plan their wedding, in which case split up the tasks into equal sections of weeks or months depending on how long you have.

As soon as possible/12 months to go

- ☐ Tell friends and family and make newspaper announcements.
- ☐ Decide on a possible date.
- ☐ Find your venue and book a celebrant but don't announce the date until you have written confirmation of both.
- ☐ Set a realistic budget for everything and work out where the money is coming from.
- ☐ Decide what you personally are responsible for. The groom generally looks after the costs for the ceremony, the music, the bride's ring, transport, the first night hotel and the honeymoon.
- ☐ Decide on the guest list.
- ☐ Choose your best man – he needs to be supportive and organised – and your ushers.

9 months to go

- ☐ Organise the engagement party.
- ☐ If you are worried about looking good, start a fitness regime about now.
- ☐ Start looking into key suppliers such as:
  - florists
  - photographers/videographers
  - caterers
  - cake makers
  - transport
  - music/entertainment
  - stationery suppliers
  - drinks suppliers.

6 months to go

- ☐ Discuss with the best man what kind of stag night you would like and who you want to invite.
- ☐ If you are having them made, order your wedding rings.
- ☐ Decide on your major suppliers for things such as your stationery, cake and flowers.

4 months to go

- [ ] Choose your outfits and hire any that need to be hired to allow enough time for alterations to be carried out.
- [ ] Confirm transport arrangements with your best man.

3 months to go

- [ ] Arrange a second meeting with your minister, priest or rabbi to discuss the service and agree a date for the publication of banns or give notice of the marriage to the superintendent registrar.
- [ ] Book your first night hotel and honeymoon.
- [ ] Check passports and have any necessary inoculations.
- [ ] Organise your gift list.
- [ ] Organise any maps etc. to be included with the invitations and then send your invitations.
- [ ] Finalise the menu.
- [ ] If you are having one, book a DJ or band.
- [ ] Check with your bride that she is coping with everything and, if she's not, help her. Plus make time to go on a date together and agree not to talk about the wedding.

2 months to go

- [ ] Reconfirm all bookings.
- [ ] Choose and buy presents for attendants; order bouquets for your and your fiancée's mother.
- [ ] Think about your seating plan.

4 weeks to go

- [ ] Make sure everyone involved in the wedding knows what's happening when and what time they're supposed to arrive.
- [ ] Arrange a lift to the airport, if necessary.
- [ ] Write and practise your speech.
- [ ] Chase any guests who still haven't replied.
- [ ] Mentally prepare yourself for the stag night…

3 weeks to go

- [ ] Pack for your honeymoon and order travellers' cheques and some foreign currency
- [ ] Confirm the final number of guests with your caterer.

1 week to go

- [ ] Attend the rehearsal.
- [ ] Make sure you have confirmed all arrangements in writing.
- [ ] Practise your speech.
- [ ] Learn your vows so you can look at your bride and not the celebrant as you say them.
- [ ] Collect hired outfits.
- [ ] Make sure your best man and ushers have tried on outfits, as well as accessories such as cufflinks.

1 day to go

- [ ] Help decorate the venue, if necessary.
- [ ] Check the weather forecast so you know whether to get the umbrellas out and keep the hood up on the convertible.
- [ ] Have the honeymoon luggage – including documents, tickets and passports – delivered to the reception venue.
- [ ] In the evening, relax over a beer with your best man – not too many though.
- [ ] Set your alarm.

The big day

- [ ] Have a hearty breakfast.
- [ ] Scrub up well.
- [ ] Call the bride and tell her you love her.
- [ ] Make sure the bride's wedding day present has been delivered.

☐ Check you have the following:
- your buttonhole
- a change of clothes for the next day
- emergency spare change
- your speech notes
- thank-you gifts
- your going-away car keys if you are driving
- your house keys.

☐ Make your way to the ceremony, allowing plenty of time.

The rest of the day…

The important bit is finished with and after your speech you can sit back and let your best man take charge.

- Keep your speech short and simple and remember to thank the bride's parents for their lovely daughter and also to thank your parents, the guests, the best man and the bridesmaids. Give out presents to both sets of parents and all the attendants. Remember to say something exclusively to the bride about how happy you are today.
- Relax… Your main job is done. Enjoy yourself and look after your new wife. Let the best man look after any minor problems – that's what he's there for.

From this day forward…

- When you get back from your honeymoon you might find that both you and your new wife suffer from the post-honeymoon blues. Go for a weekend away or a few nice meals out to try and fight it.
- Open all your presents and then write thank you cards.
- Get your photographs back from the photographer and choose the best prints for your album.
- Don't let the romance slip – say 'I love you' at least once a day, make time to go on proper dates together, remember that good old fashioned hand-holding should never be underrated and make sure you make a big splash about your first anniversary of married life together.

16

Useful Contacts

www.youandyourwedding.co.uk – whether you want to work out your budget, arrange your seating plan, find great suppliers or point your bride in the direction of the chat rooms it will save you tons of time and effort.

Gifts for your best man/ushers

Boy's Stuff
www.boysstuff.co.uk

Fire Box
www.firebox.com

Framed Share
www.framedshare.co.uk

I Want One Of Those
www.iwantoneofthose.com

Paramount Zone
www.paramountzone.co.uk

Simon Carter
www.simoncarter.net

Honeymoons

Abercrombie & Kent
0845 070 0610
www.abercrombiekent.co.uk

British Airways Holidays
0870 850 9850
www.britishairways.com

British Airways Travel Clinic
www.britishairways/travel/health

Caribtours
020 7751 0660
www.caribtours.co.uk

Elegant Resorts
01244 897222
www.elegantresorts.co.uk

First Choice
www.firstchoice.co.uk

The Foreign Office
www.fco.gov.uk

ITC Classics
01244 355527
www.itcclassics.co.uk

Kuoni
www.kuoni.co.uk

Seasons in Style
www.seasonsinstyle.co.uk

Thomas Cook Signature
0870 443 4440
www.tcsignature.com

Thomson
www.thomson.co.uk

Virgin Holidays
www.virginholidays.com

Men's spa treatments

Bliss (London)
www.blisslondon.co.uk

Dandy Brown's (Leeds)
www.dandybrowns.com

Dress2kill Grooming (London)
www.dress2killgrooming.com

Elemis (nationwide)
01278 727830 www.elemis.com

Elizabeth Arden (nationwide)
www.reddoorspas.com

E'Spa Spas (nationwide)
www.espainternational.co.uk

Gentlemen's Tonic (London)
020 7297 4343
www.gentlemenstonic.com

Geo F Trumpers (London)
www.trumpers.com

Jason Shankey Male Grooming
(Belfast and London)
www.jasonshankey.com

Nickel Spa (London)
www.nickelspalondon.co.uk

Pankhurst at Alfred Dunhill (London)
020 7290 8636

The Refinery (London)
www.the-refinery.com

Space.NK (London)
www.spacenk.co.uk

Menswear –
to hire and buy

Austin Reed (nationwide)
www.austinreed.co.uk

Brooks Brothers (London)
020 7256 5195

Burton Menswear (nationwide)
0870 606 9666
www.burtonmenswear.co.uk

Charles Tyrwhitt (nationwide)
www.ctshirts.co.uk

Daks (nationwide)
020 7409 4000 www.daks.com

Debenhams (nationwide)
020 7408 4444
www.debenhams.co.uk

Ede & Ravenscroft
www.edeandravenscroft.co.uk

Eton Shirts (nationwide)
www.etonshirts.co.uk

Favourbrook (nationwide)
020 7491 2337
www.favourbrook.com

Gieves & Hawkes (nationwide)
www.gievesandhawkes.com

Hackett (nationwide)
www.hackett.com

Hire Society (nationwide)
0870 780 2003
www.hire-society.com

House of Fraser (nationwide)
0870 160 7270

John Lewis (nationwide)
www.johnlewis.com

Marc Wallace (London)
020 7731 4575
www.marcwallace.com

Massimo Dutti (nationwide)
www.massimodutti.com

Moss Bros Hire (nationwide)
020 7447 7200
www.mossbroshire.co.uk

Ozwald Boateng (nationwide)
www.ozwaldboateng.co.uk

Pal Zileri
020 7493 9711

Paul Smith (nationwide)
020 7836 7828
www.paulsmith.co.uk

Pierre Cardin (nationwide)
01788 551995

Pronuptia (nationwide)
01273 323046
www.pronuptia.co.uk

Ted Baker (nationwide)
www.tedbaker.co.uk

Thomas Pink (nationwide)
020 7498 3882
www.thomaspink.co.uk

Timothy Everest (London)
020 7629 6236

TM Lewin (nationwide)
www.tmlewin.co.uk

Turnbull & Asser (London)
www.turnbullandasser.co.uk

Young Bride & Groom (nationwide)
www.youngbrideandgroom.co.uk

Young's Hire at Suits You and Suit
Direct (nationwide)
020 8327 3005
www.youngs-hire.co.uk

Photography

British Institute of Professional
Photography
www.bipp.com

Master Photographers Association
www.thempa.com

Religious groups and register offices

Baptists Union
01235 517700

British Humanist Association
020 7079 3580
www.humanism.org.uk

Church of England
020 7898 1000
www.cofe.anglican.org

Church of Scotland
0131 225 5722

General Register Office (GRO) for
England and Wales
0151 471 4200
www.ons.gov.uk

GRO for Guernsey
01481 725277

GRO for Jersey
01534 502335

GRO for Northern Ireland
028 9025 2000

GRO for Scotland
0131 314 4447

Greek Archdiocese
020 7723 4787

Jewish Marriage Council
020 8203 6311

Marriage Care – Catholic
020 7371 1341
www.marriagecare.org.uk

Methodist Church
020 7222 8010

United Reformed Church
020 7916 2020

Speeches

MJ Consulting Speech Making
Courses (Edinburgh)
0131 466 6051

Utter Wit
www.utterwit.co.uk

Wedding Speech Builder
www.weddingspeechbuilder.com

Write 4 Me
www.write4me.co.uk

Stag nights

Big Weekends
www.bigweekends.com

Blokes Only
www.blokesonly.com

Buy A Gift
www.buyagift.co.uk

Chilli Sauce
www.chillisauce.co.uk

Extreme Activities
www.extreme-activities.com

Go Ape
www.goape.co.uk

Great Experience Days
www.greatexperiencedays.co.uk

Knights Of Middle England
www.knightsofmiddleengland.co.uk

Last Night of Freedom
www.lastnightoffreedom.co.uk

Maximise
www.maximise.co.uk

National Karting Association
www.nationalkarting.co.uk

Red Letter Days
www.redletterdays.co.uk

Red Seven Leisure
www.redsevenleisure.co.uk

The Stag Company
www.thestagcompany.com

The Stag and Hen Company
www.thestagandhencompany.co.uk

Stag Web
www.stagweb.co.uk

Stag Weekends
www.stagweekends.com

Track Days
www.trackdays.co.uk

Toastmasters

National Association of Toastmasters
‘ 0845 838 2814
www.natuk.com

Transport companies

AK Vintage
www.akvintage.co.uk

American Dreams
www.americandreams.co.uk

Antique Auto Agency
www.antique-auto-agency.co.uk

Blue Triangle Buses
www.bluetrianglebuses.com

Cabair Helicopters
www.cabairhelicopters.com

Cops and Cabbies
www.copsandcabbies.com

Courtyard Carriages
www.courtyardcarriages.co.uk

East Midlands Helicopters
www.helicopter-services.co.uk

Elite Helicopters
www.elitehelicopters.co.uk

Flights 4 All
www.flights4all.com

Historic & Classic Car Hirers' Guild
www.hchg.co.uk

Karma Kabs
www.karmakabs.com

Lord Cars
www.lordcars.co.uk

The Marriage Carriage Company
www.themarriagecarriage
company.co.uk

Memory Lane
www.memorylane.co.uk

The Open Road
www.theopenroad.co.uk

Star Car Hire
www.starcarhire.co.uk

Starlite Limos
www.starlitelimos.co.uk

Wedding Carriage Company
www.wedding-carriage.co.uk

Weather forecast

www.metoffice.gov.uk,
www.bbc.co.uk/weather

Photograph Acknowledgements

Introduction: page 8 Moss Bros (020 7447 7200, www.mossbros.co.uk)

Chapter 1: page 10 David Jones/Good Housekeeping UK; page 11 Moss Bros (020 7447 7200, www.mossbros.co.uk)

Chapter 2: page 18 Mike McClafferty/She UK; page 19 Cosmopolitan UK; page 22 Matthew Shave/Cosmopolitan UK

Chapter 3: page 24 Studio 21/Zest; page 25 Alison Offley (www.alison offley.com); page 27 Mason Photography (www.masonphotography. co.uk); page 28 Freeman Photographics (www.freemanphotographics.co.uk)

Chapter 4: page 37 Craig Prentis (01892 536014, www.craig prentis.co.uk); page 38 Moss Bros (020 7447 7200, www.mossbros.co.uk); page 39 Mason Photography (www.masonphotography.co.uk); page 43 Winifred Heinze/She UK

Chapter 5: page 44 The Grove, Hertfordshire (01923 807807); page 45 Mason Photography (www.mason photography.co.uk); page 46 Sian Irvine/You & Your Wedding UK; page 47 Stoke Park Club, Buckinghamshire (01753 717171); page 48 Ryan Sullivan/You & Your Wedding UK; page 51 British Airways London Eye (0870 220 2223)

Chapter 6: page 52 Ede & Ravenscroft (020 7405 3906); page 53 Phil Evans (www.philevansphoto.co.uk); page 54 Pal Zileri (www.palzileri.com); page 55 Mason Photography (www.mason photography.co.uk); page 56 Oliver Sweeney (www.oliversweeney.com); Duchamp (020 7243 3970): page 57 Marc Wallace (020 7731 4575); page 59 Nickel Spa (www.nickelspa london.co.uk); pages 60 and 61 Sandy Lane, Barbados (www.sandylane.com)

Chapter 7: page 63 Rachel Barnes/You & Your Wedding UK; page 64 Michael Paul/Good Housekeeping UK; page 65 Peter Dürkes; page 67 Peter Dürkes;

page 69 Debbie Wilkinson (01482 644759, www.debbiewilkinson.co.uk); page 70 Star Car Hire (www.starcar hire.co.uk), Freeman Photographics (www.freemanphotographics.co.uk); page 72 Freeman Photographics (www.freemanphotographics.co.uk); page 75 Page Teahan (01258 817961); page 77 Rachel Barnes Photography (www.rachelbarnes.co.uk); page 79 Sian Irvine/You & Your Wedding UK; page 80 Hotel Du Vin, Brighton (www.hotelduvin.com)

Chapter 8: page 82 Studio 21/Zest UK; page 86 Buy A Gift (www.buyagift. co.uk); page 89 Biz/Cosmopolitan UK

Chapter 9: page 90 Lovegrove Photography (www.lovegrove weddings.com); page 91 Getty Images; page 92 Moss Bros (020 7447 7200, www.mossbros.co.uk); page 95 Photolibrary.com

Chapter 10: page 96 Getty Images; page 98 Studio 21/Zest; page 100 Getty Images

Chapter 11: page 103 One&Only St Geran, Mauritius (www.oneandonly resorts.com); page 104 One&Only Le Touessrok, Mauritius (www.oneand onlyresorts.com); page 106 Ulusaba, South Africa (www.virginlimited edition.co.uk)

Chapter 12: page 108 Lovegrove Photography (www.lovegrove weddings.com); page 110 Getty Images; page 113 Bailey Cooper (01904 416684, www.baileycooper.co.uk); page 115 Paul Cudmore (www.proshoot. co.uk)

Chapter 13: page 117 Michael Blyth (www.michaelblyth.co.uk); page 119 Moss Bros (020 7447 7200, www.moss bros.co.uk); page 120 Rachel Barnes Photography (www.rachelbarnes.co.uk)

Chapter 14: page 124 You & Your Wedding UK

Chapter 15: page 132 Moss Bros Hire (020 7447 7200, www.mossbros.co.uk)

Photograph Acknowledgements

For Your Notes

Planning notes

For Your Notes

Outfit notes

Budget notes

Honeymoon notes

Index

Page numbers in **bold** indicate major references

Index

Index